WITHDRAWN

Give Me That
ONLINE RELIGION

Give Me That
ONLINE RELIGION

BRENDA E. BRASHER

JOSSEY-BASS
A Wiley Company
San Francisco

Jossey-Bass books and products are available through most bookstores. To contact Jossey-Bass directly,
call (888) 378-2537, fax to (800) 605-2665, or visit our Website at www.josseybass.com.

Substantial discounts on bulk quantities of Jossey-Bass books are available to corporations, professional
associations, and other organizations. For details and discount information, contact the special sales
department at Jossey-Bass.

Printed in the United States of America.
Text design by Lisa Buckley.

Library of Congress Cataloging-in-Publication Data

Brasher, Brenda E., date.
    Give me that online religion / Brenda E. Brasher.
        p. cm.
Includes bibliographical references and index.
    ISBN 0-7879-4579-X (alk. paper)
    1. Religion—Computer network resources. 2. Internet—Religious aspects.
3. Cyberspace—Religious aspects. I. Title.
    BL37 .B73 2001
        025.06′2—dc21   00-11190

FIRST EDITION
HB Printing   10 9 8 7 6 5 4 3 2 1

CONTENTS

Disclaimer

We know that many of the Websites listed in this book no longer exist. That is the nature of the Web. However, religion is alive and well on the Internet. See the author's Website, http://www.brendabrasher.com for a list of current Websites.

For Jason, who introduced me to my first computer,

And for Michael, who together with me found love via one

Acknowledgments

Due to the accidents of time and history, I wrote this book during tumultuous times for me personally as well as for U.S. society at large. The unexpected and sudden death of my mother midway through the writing process brought everything other than basic essentials to a halt for several months. Then, a huge sway of enthusiasm for the popular turn of the millennium pulled me into a plethora of television appearances and conferences. Through these upheavals, my extraordinary writing agent, Katharine Sands, proved herself a friend and confidante far beyond what I had any right to expect. She was wise enough to give me the freedom to mourn. She also was wise enough to pull me back from mourning into productive life when the time was right. Katherine is a modern muse to whom I owe considerable thanks.

Second, I owe a huge debt of gratitude to Sarah Polster, my editor at Jossey-Bass. Sarah's patient encouragement was a vital tonic throughout. The quiet conversations we had in her office, on the San Francisco ferry, and in her peaceful home with her lovely daughter playing around us were an important factor in helping me find and cross the bridge between my earliest ideas for this book and what it has finally become.

During the years that this book germinated in my mind, other conversation partners also proved quite inspiring. Foremost among them is Richard Landes, whose funny and keen wit is a true treasure. Very early on, a number of people played key roles in encouraging me to think and write about this topic, including Jan Fernback, Sam Smith, Lin Collette, and Diane Winston. I am especially thankful to the American Academy of Religion's New Technologies Task Force, which strove hard every year to provide settings at the AAR annual meeting where issues of religion and technology could be addressed. The intellectual streams that feed into a work such as this are quite varied. Stephen O'Leary was enormously helpful in the area of millennial studies. Jon Bienz steered me toward valuable resources in the area of medieval time.

I also want to thank Jossey-Bass, an amazing publishing company in terms of the way it got behind this book. In addition to Sarah Polster, I wish to thank Bruce Emmer, whose wry editorial comments made me laugh even as I worked harder to improve the text, and Chandrika Madhavan, who tracked me down across continents to coordinate my interactions with the J-B organization. I was deeply impressed by the incredibly hard work of Joanne Clapp Fullagar and Andrea Flint, in charge of producing the book. Accolades are due to the talented design team of Paula Goldstein and Lisa Buckley, who developed the book's impressive visuals. Accolades are also due to the J-B marketing team of Mark Kerr, Robert Heckman, Jennifer Bendery, and Adrienne Biggs, whose understanding of the contemporary passion for thoughtful explorations into human spirituality fueled the book's introduction to the wider public.

January 2001   Brenda E. Brasher
Alliance, Ohio

Give Me That
ONLINE RELIGION

A Revolution in the Making: Spiritual Wonder Goes Online

To interact via a computer monitor with an online Hindu temple is a profoundly different religious experience.

Near the top of a narrow road that threads around a small mountain located near the city of Bangalore in southwestern India, a small Hindu temple dedicated to Kali hugs the ground. As with most Hindu places of worship, the exterior of the white stone temple is completely covered with elaborate carvings depicting goddesses and gods deporting themselves in accord with scenes from cherished sacred Hindu tales. People wait patiently for hours in a long line to get inside, into the temple's heart, to be near an image of Kali.

With slick black limbs in supple pose, Kali sits in the center of the temple, looking as if she had been sculpted of molten ebony and would burst into flame were it not for two hammered silver cuffs that simultaneously adorn and cool off her volatility. Multicolored twinkling lights positioned around Kali give her a sparkling, rainbow frame. Directly in front of the image, a circular brass tray holds glowing embers that emit fat puffs of gray smoke—offerings to Kali's *Shakti* (sacred energy).

Around Kali, devotees stretch out their arms and call to her in singsong prayers, while in a nearby alcove Brahmin priests chant the Sanskrit verses of a private *puja* (worship) for those gathered near. The fragrance of flower and fruit *puja* offerings hangs heavily in the air.

Worshiping Kali at the temple involves sounds, smells, tastes, and sights that leave newcomers breathless, absorbing them in an encounter with the numinous, the sacred unknown—a transcendent otherness that attracts and frightens at the same time.

To interact via a computer monitor with an online Hindu temple is a profoundly different religious experience. Consider, for instance, a Web page titled Digital Avatar. Without leaving your desk chair, you can visit this virtual temple. The page opens to reveal not a temple building but rather a small, stunningly rendered image of a white-faced Shiva framed in black. Moving into the site, you discover a menu of worship experiences. Under a smiling Shiva mouth, hyperlinked text invites you to click on it to savor Shiva's cosmic delights. Other links offer "take-away" religious experiences. You can download Shiva's image for later attempts to encounter his *Shakti*. If it's meditative bliss you seek, you can download the *aum*, the mystical utterance of Vedic praise that expresses and affirms the totality of creation. For those who need or want visual stimulation as well, a QuickTime movie file with accompanying sound allows you to meditate to an eerie, mystical, rapid alternation of Shiva images.

In light of the fact that the Digital Avatar site was produced during cyberspace's infancy, it was a marvelously foresighted effort to construct the sacred electronically. *Imaginative* absorption into the numinous may occasionally be sparked by its provocative multimediated construction. Yet its ability to stimulate *physical* absorption into the numinous is highly limited.

To contrast Digital Avatar with the Kali temple, in the former the journey to the site is gone. There is no wait to get into the temple. There is no interaction with other pilgrims en route. The temple itself is gone. The heavy smell of flower and fruit offerings has vanished. In sum, in the transition from temple to screen, a radical alteration of the sense stimulation integral to Hindu worship has silently taken place. Consequently, the religious experience itself has been altered. The numinous, or holy, experience that cyberspace makes possible by way of Digital Avatar is almost entirely an affair of the mind. This stands in huge contrast to the immersion of mind and body in the numinous of an actual visit to the Kali temple.

Still, the Kali temple itself imposes limits. Only a select number of people beyond those who live in the immediate vicinity can readily visit the temple. Given its smallish size, a mere fifty or so can enter the temple at any one time. At the temple, novice worshipers may gaze without comprehension upon the iconography meant to summon the gods' presence. None of these limits apply to Digital Avatar. Its hyperlinked visual elements enable visitors who see an unfamiliar image or sound to learn all about it in their own language. Whereas a thousand may travel to the temple of Kali in one month, that many and more can visit Digital Avatar in one day.

The mere fact that a person travels to a place is no guarantee that she or he will fully experience it (as any parent or guardian who has gone to synagogue, church, or mosque and taken along a two-year-old can attest). Digital Avatar can be visited at two in the afternoon or three in the morning—when the computer is free, the weather is awful, the car is not running, the children are in bed. Whenever time for the contemplative arises, online religion is there. All it takes is a momentary visit to cyberspace, the unexpectedly novel terrain of human spirituality.

Cyberspace as the Site of Online Religion

Cyberspace is a fiction of public etiquette that orients people in a virtual environment. An abstract idea with electronic components, cyberspace identifies the expanse, if not the time, where those communicating by means of computers believe and act as if they are. A partly communal "where" fantasy, cyberspace is the sum total of the millions of mental maps people draw on when online to determine where they are. At the start of the new millennium, the best-known use of cyberspace is for commerce. Whatever else it may be, cyberspace is our first global, virtual mall. Surging excitement over cyberspace as a commercial locale produced some of the late twentieth century's wealthiest individuals. For a time, futuristic allure overrode unproven profitability to make online stocks soar.

Yet one of the best-kept secrets of cyberspace is the surprising amount of religious practice that takes place there. My own explorations have revealed more than one million online religion Websites in operation. They encompass every major religious tradition in the world, most new religious groups, and innumerable social movements that function as de facto religions for their followers. The sites and activities that make up online religion are intriguing, delightful, and at times disturbing. The central goal of this book is to introduce the phenomenon, along with certain interpretive frameworks that may help make sense of it all.

A low-key political argument winds throughout the book as well. I contend that online religion is a crucial contemporary cultural outlet for our meaning heritage from the past. Bringing religion into the global arena, online religion ensures that humanity's religious acumen is kept alive and positions that heritage to maximize its relevance for future generations. Most important, for all the risks entailed, the wisdom Web pages and holy hyperlinks that are the stuff of online religion possess the potential to make a unique contribution to global fellowship in the frequently volatile area of interreligious understanding. Fueling the trend that widespread mobility began, cyberspace diminishes the relevance of location for religious identity. As it widens the social foundation of religious life, cyberspace erodes the

> Fueling the trend that widespread mobility began, cyberspace diminishes the relevance of location for religious identity. As it widens the social foundation of religious life, cyberspace erodes the basis from which religion contributes to the destructive dynamics of xenophobia.

basis from which religion contributes to the destructive dynamics of xenophobia. In the process, it lessens potential interreligious hatred. Because of this, just as "real" religions are acknowledged and supported in the form of tax abatements, one political argument this book makes is that online religion should receive comparable public acknowledgment and support. Its successful development harbors important hope for the future of civil society.

A Little Definition

Before plunging into the extraordinary adventure of online religion, it may be helpful to define *cyberspace* more carefully. Evoked by the intermesh of computer hardware and software, telephone or cable lines, and the human imagination, cyberspace is at once monolithic and diverse. The monolithic aspects of cyberspace derive from its technologies and protocols. Their consistency makes computer-mediated communication (CMC) possible. At the same time, cyberspace is necessarily pluralistic. It has material diversity from the variety of hardware and software people use to access it. It has psychological diversity from the variety of human users who enter it.

That people inhabit cyberspace when they go online is, to a degree, a whimsical turn of events on the part of computer users. But they have not invented cyberspace totally on their own. Computer hardware and software organizations, along with "dot-com" companies of varied ilk, have worked hard to construct the Freudian illusion that is cyberspace. Sound and dazzling color imbue cyberspace with seductive virtual substance. Like the childhood dream of a perfect parent, the key illusion of cyberspace is that it is continuously available and can answer our every desire. Want a new car? Go online. Want companionship? Go online. Want to know what the weather is like in Antarctica? Go online. Want to know whether we are receiving signals from another planet? Go online. And people respond. Each day, millions of computer users engage in the repetitive acts of communal imagination that bring cyberspace into being.

Among the genres of human fantasy, cyberspace most closely resembles myth. It is a public story that expresses widely held values and beliefs. The popularity accorded this semi-imaginary locale gives it more symbolic weight than countless actual places have. Believed in by millions, cyberspace is real in its consequences if not in its geography. In cyberspace, we see the inaugural instance of global interactive relations. Through it, we have at our fingertips a form of community that could include the whole world. If fully realized on a macro scale, the global interactive fellowships that cyberspace supports could alter our assumptions about what constitutes community and make obsolete the boundaries of the modern nation-state. On a micro scale, it could mean that at the edges of life no one ever need be alone. But thanks to its capacity to produce enormous wealth, cyberspace is quickly becoming commodified. Its mythic potential is being electronically etched over by banner ads, "cookies" (the small text files that some Website you visit create on your own computer's hard drive), and push mail.

At Home in Cyberspace

It is a notable human trait that people who inhabit a territory extend its significance by attaching invisible meanings to its physical features. The imagination instrumentally aids our ability to relate to every abode. A good example is the large white rock that sits next to the outdoor tennis courts at the small liberal arts college where I teach. Three feet wide and two feet tall, the white rock is simply a rock to campus visitors; but to the students, the rock is a site of highly contested meaning. During the day, it is a mineral billboard that advertises the slogan or logo of some school group. According to local custom, no one touches the rock during the day.

But once night falls, a band of painters from a campus group surreptitiously paints the rock with a message for the next day. Some nights, the white rock is painted over three times as bands of painters vie to be the ones whose message the rock carries the next day. Visitors physically see the white rock. Culturally, it is invisible to them. But for insiders, knowledge and imagination create a thick web of meanings around the rock that frame and color it. That makes all the difference.

To a certain extent, the grids of invisible meaning that people lay upon cyberspace differ little from how my students relate to the white rock—except that my students are, at least, restrained by the rock. The virtual terrain of cyberspace has few, if any, consistent physical objects; consequently, more than most places of heightened cultural meaning, cyberspace is substantially determined by the imaginations of those who engage it. To one person, it is a swirl of mind and emotions awakened by fervently dancing electrically charged elements. To another, it is the mental oasis one enters upon hearing the placid hum of computer processing and tapping keystrokes, accompanied by the visual stimuli of ever-changing combinations of electronic symbols, icons, and images. In short, there can be as many cyberspaces as there are people online at a given time.

This variety sets the stage for the intense conflicts over the virtual world that regularly arise. Is cyberspace a public square or a carnival? Is it a place where common decency applies or where all rules are off? Citizens and politicians contend among themselves and with each other over whether cyberspace should be—or even can be—safe, frightening, sexual, playful, violent, serene, profane, sacred, carefully fenced in, or regulated at all. Absent a viable concord over virtual decorum, conflicts flare online, in law courts, and in legislative bodies over what can and should take place in cyberspace. None of this slows the breakneck expansion of cyberspace. Individuals, schools, corporations, governments, and religious groups are busily erecting virtual contributions to a place that did not exist half a century ago, even though they do not agree on exactly what kind of place it is.

According to British philosopher and mathematician Alfred North Whitehead, religion is what people do with their solitude.[1] Rabbi Lawrence Zierler, of the Cleveland Jewish Community Center, gives a similarly intrinsic definition for religion; it is, he contends, "a matter of the heart."[2] To the deeply pious, religion is the main activity through which one's deepest, ultimate concerns are expressed. Yet a quick drive down almost any major artery in the United States quickly dispels the idea that religion is an activity consigned to the private. In block after block, sacred buildings of all sorts and sizes color the urban, suburban, and rural landscape of America like scattered wildflowers. A quick read of almost any daily newspaper similarly dispels the idea that religion remains easily within the bounds of the heart. Most of this country's most intransigent social controversies—abortion rights, the death penalty, the content of public education—are fueled by citizens' religious beliefs; those who hold them would like the beliefs to be actualized into public policy for all.

This book is not neutral about religion. Its central thesis is that religious expression in cyberspace should be a protected and supported use of the virtual domain.

Born of the cold war paranoid desire for indestructible military communications, cyberspace came of age in the United States in academia and later in the realm of commerce in the closing decades of the twentieth century. That something spawned by the military, cultivated by academia, and colonized by commerce would come to house an enormous quantity of sites dedicated to religious expression is an amazing, if little known, fact. From the Vatican to Buddhist mediation to the Dark Lair of Infinite Evil, online religion flourishes.

Scant attention has been paid to this development, and almost no consideration has been given to why and how people turned to computer-mediated technologies to find or create the spiritual experiences they craved. The ethnographic depictions of religion in cyberspace spread throughout this book are intended to address this oversight. They take you on a textual tour of cyberspace spirituality, calling attention to the fact that virtual temples and churches dot the landscape of cyberspace almost as much as online flower shops and virtual bookstores do. A segment of the religiously inclined populace has deemed cyberspace a viable outlet for its religious interests and made it the virtual repository of a tremendous outpouring of religious enthusiasm and desire.

This book is not neutral about religion. Its central thesis—that religious expression in cyberspace should be a protected and supported use of the virtual domain—is the logical extension of two interrelated, foundational, proreligion contentions. The first is that religious people and their traditions make a valuable, necessary contribution to civil society, while acknowledging that this is not always the case and that no one tradition does so perfectly at all times. An extension of this first contention is that religious tradition offers a rich, incomparable meaning resource—necessary ballast to individual identity. The second major contention is that online religion is crucial to and positive for the future of religion. It is a vital cultural vehicle necessary for the emergence of religious experience and expression relevant to a future society. Against the onslaught of commercialization in cyberspace, online religion could rapidly become an Internet endangered species. This book not only documents and analyzes the phenomenon of online religion but also argues for its public reservation as an integral part of our global future.

The Persistence of Religious Plurality

No one religious tradition has ever completely articulated humanity's longing for, encounter with, and understanding of the transcendent—those aspects of lived experience that seem to extend beyond our individual, finite existence. Religion exists in the plural; hence it is addressed here in a pluralistic, inclusive sense. As imperfect as it is, religion makes a meaningful contribution to civil society not offered by other organizations. Traditional religions thrust forward through time ideas and values, rituals and organizations of the past. They conserve and stabilize civil society as it confronts the challenges of its era that politics, society, and climate yield up. New religious groups perform a different but also important function. Typically incorporating elements of established traditions, new religions capsulize the values and ideas of emerging cultural paradigms. Whereas traditional religions stabilize existing cultural patterns, new religions stabilize and lend coherence to the culturally new.

During cultural shifts, both established and new religions play important roles. Older religions keep account of heritage and seek its recognition and proper expression in the present. New religions provide the social framework for instilling new values into the new ways of life.

What causes cultural shift? Historically, the causes have been complex and multiple, with technology a key player. Whether it is, as David Landes has pointedly argued,[3] that new technology does not cause revolution but is valued by the society whose revolutionary values it expresses or whether technology itself generates revolution, the interrelationship (if not the causality) of new technology and cultural shift is clear.

When a new technology unleashes massive cultural change, the challenge to traditional religion is immense. In the West, established and new religions alike have vied to fulfill their conserving and articulating functions by exploiting innovation in communication technology that accompanied cultural change. The printing press, radio, film, and television each attracted religious virtuosos who drew on the innovation in communication to conserve past values or express new ones amid the new landscape wrought by cultural change. As the latest site of cultural challenge and change, online religions (traditional and new) represent a stabilizing influence in the virtual domain.

Religion, Cultural Change, and the Revolutionary Importance of Online Religion

Clearly, religions change over time. For proof, consider the number of ancient religious practices that have vanished from our daily lives. From burying the living spouses and servants of rulers to die along with them so that a ruler can enjoy their company in the next world to creating cave paintings to guarantee a successful bison hunt, activities in which our prehistoric ancestors widely engaged as an expression of their spiritual wonder are no more.

Consider as well the number of religious practices readily accepted today that our forebears never dreamed of. A videotaped ceremony, an interreligious gathering, or a congregational Web page are all common elements of spirituality in the new millennium, but they would have puzzled, and possibly horrified, our ancestors of a few hundred years ago.

As the opening comparison between a "real-world" and virtual Hindu holy site revealed, online religion triggers notable changes in religious experience that cannot help but transform the character of religion itself. A number of historical parallels support this assessment. To consider them, it is helpful to keep in mind that online religion is a type of spiritual activity made possible by the popularization of new media technologies. Viewing online religion from this perspective brings its revolutionary potential into focus, although why this is the case may not immediately be clear. Certainly, entertainment, profit, business needs, and defense goals have all been more instrumental in inspiring communication innovation in the late twentieth century than religion has. Even though religious communication has rarely, if ever, been the driving factor behind the development of new communication technologies, innovative religious thinkers have been at the forefront of those exploiting new communication technology to disseminate their ideas. In the process, they provoke some of the most significant changes that religions have undergone.

For Christianity of the Latin West, Martin Luther's use of the printing press provides a striking example. As changing economic and social conditions in late-fifteenth-century Germany made reading and writing more necessary and thus more valuable, print shops spread. By eliminating the costly time of the copyist that had until then been necessary for the mass production of documents, print shops brought efficiency to commerce while satisfying the new paperwork needs of a modernizing society.

Little was it suspected that popularization of this communication technology would transform European religion, yet that is precisely what happened. As the printing press made the information formerly limited to rare and expensive texts more available and affordable, the fledgling industry gave birth to a new, more inclusive public. This in turn invited fifteenth-century Europeans to re-envision their understanding of community: who constitutes it, who can speak to and for it, who should or must be heard, what it is important to know.

As the printing press altered the prevailing notion of what constituted a public forum, it also undermined the traditional mode of authoritative speech. Before the technology of the printing press became widespread, religious authority in a mostly Christian Europe was solidly anchored in the hierarchically organized Roman Catholic Church. What was acceptably religious and what constituted heresy—the main building blocks of religion—was decided by religious authorities and trickled down to the populace on a need-to-know basis. With the advent of the printing press, Luther and other Christian dissidents had the means to challenge conventional religious norms—means that Luther, especially, exploited to the fullest. Referring to Luther as the first modern propagandist, historian Mark Edwards added up the number of pamphlets each proto-Protestant published in the early 1500s and found that Luther not only outpublished all other dissenters in his era but outpublished the entire collection of antidissidents marshaled by the Roman Catholic Church![4]

Little was it suspected that popularization of printing would transform European religion, yet that is precisely what happened.

The consequences of Luther's reform propaganda were formidable for religion. Organizationally, it launched a major stream of Christianity that eventually became known as Protestantism and inspired a reformulation of the Latin Catholic tradition as well. Other changes were equally profound. Luther's attempt to subvert hierarchical channels of authority led him to write more and more of his persuasive pamphlets in the vernacular, the language of the people (in his case, an early version of German). But as arguments about such important public issues as church authority were advanced in a popular language, this implied that the arguments were the concern of common people, that what they thought about such things mattered. There can be no more revolutionary idea than this, as Luther—to his rather patrician regret—found out.

In Judaism, the printing press had a similar revolutionary effect. The principal text of Jewish mysticism, the Zohar, was printed and broadly distributed during this same period; coupled with production of codex versions of the Torah, this placed the tools necessary to construct populist Jewish movements in the hands of a wide Jewish audience.

Still, from this evidence it is not clear whether communications technology alone can alter the future of religion. Perhaps the key element is the radical innovator, who employs the technology for change-inducing purposes. After all, when radio, broadcast television, and cable television were introduced, they were new communication technologies that connected humanity in unprecedented ways; however, in considerable contrast to the printing press, their early impact on religion was negligible. This was not due to the absence of revolutionary potential within the technologies themselves; rather, it was the consequence of the nonrevolutionary uses to which religionists put them.

The initial religionists who adopted radio and television to communicate their message were leaders of established mainstream religious groups. Unlike Luther, these traditionalist leaders were not driven by any agenda for change. Also unlike Luther, they intended to use the new technology to bolster the status quo rather than modify it. And yet in spite of this nonrevolutionary intent, over time these technologies had a revolutionary impact. Through them, groups that had been socially marginalized, such as Christian evangelicals, garnered cultural prominence for their movement and accrued political power.

Radio and television produced other unintended changes in religion as well. With the advent of these technologies, the American general public was exposed daily to professionally produced, well-orchestrated entertainment. For religion, one consequence of this was that people soon wanted the production quality and professionalism of radio and television to be exhibited in *local* worship events. Rather than participants in a faith community, people started to think of themselves as an audience and began acting like observers at worship. The popularity of megachurches—religious groups of fifteen hundred or more—soared in part because they could afford the massive resources necessary to stage professional-quality worship. Radio and TV, seemingly innocuous in effect and used by religionists without radical purposefulness, changed the overall tone and pace of late-twentieth-century religion. Given new technology's proven ability to influence religion, the enormous success of computer-mediated communication guarantees that it will have a transformative impact on religion, although which of its characteristics will prove most influential only time will reveal.

Religion in Cyberspace and the Future of Religion

Online religion is the most portentous development for the future of religion to come out of the twentieth century. Making this claim is a daring gamble, for predicting the future of faith is a risky endeavor. If past attempts are a reliable guide, forecasting the future of religion is a pastime equivalent to bungee-jumping off a bridge using a badly frayed cord. Bodies lie broken on the rocks below.

In the West, the broken bodies of failed futurists include a number of illustrious intellectuals. One of the most famous is Sigmund Freud. In the late 1920s, Freud penned an impassioned prediction of the demise of religion. In *The Future of an Illusion*,[5] he characterized religion as a human wish projected upon the universe. He contended that the illusion would vanish with proper education. By the late 1990s, public education had spread tremendously, yet religion did not vanish. Instead, it thrived. Ironically, the increase in education, which Freud advocated, produced an eclipse of the thinker's reputation rather than that of religion.

Another who boldly predicted the demise of religion was Friedrich Nietzsche. His predictions regarding the future of religion met a more rapid end than Freud's did, in part because Nietzsche's writing on religion was badly misunderstood. By using a fictional madman to proclaim that God was dead and "we have killed him,"[6] Nietzsche was contending that the idea of God was no longer a viable, living presence in human consciousness. To Nietzsche, the death of this idea had consequences. As the internalized idea of God faltered, its capacity to arbitrate human moral behavior was increasingly impaired. Its absence, he insisted, had unleashed the depravity of his age.

Popular response treated his admittedly esoteric analysis and theology of culture as if it were a police report—as if Nietzsche had taken a walk one day, come across a being named God keeled over on the sidewalk with a bullet wound through the heart, and yelled out "God is dead" to describe what he saw. Under the influence of what Alfred North

Whitehead might have described as a severe case of misplaced concreteness,[7] people dismissed Nietzsche's ideas as grossly misguided at best and hugely dangerous at worst. The widespread adoption (some would argue distortion) of Nietzsche's *Übermensch* ("superhuman") by leaders of the Third Reich proved the latter dismissal to be true and consigned his ideas to future-faith oblivion.

Religious diversity is increasing as people continue to value the particularities of their faith—even when these particularities thrust them into conflict with their neighbors.

Religious practitioners prophesying the future of religion have fared little better. A stellar pantheon of evangelical theologians has undertaken the intellectual leap of faith soothsaying, only to come to a hapless end. Predictions of the ultimate triumph of Christianity, of Islam, or of any one religious system over all others, have been disastrously misguided, as is attested by the startling diversity of religion today. Ecumenical theologians who project the future of faith have proved equally nonprescient. Here the bodies on the rocks include Wilfred Cantwell Smith, who predicted the end of religion by claiming that religion was a nonessential context within which one lived out a relationship with God or ultimate reality.[8] The victims on the rocks also include disguised ecumenical theologians such as the popular American historian of religions Huston Smith, who, in his charming and sympathetic descriptions of religions ranging from Sufi mysticism to Greek orthodoxy, attempts to persuade his readers that all religions are essentially one.[9]

In essence, both Smiths suggest that religious particularity is a distraction that calls our attention away from underlying oneness. As the twentieth century progressed, religious people en masse failed to make the prediction of either Smith come true. Religious diversity is increasing as people continue to value the particularities of their faith—even when these particularities thrust them into conflict with their neighbors. Rodney Stark, William Bainbridge, and other sociologists studying religion reveal that religious groups that strip off particularity and abandon strictness soon lose their adherents.[10] Apparently oblivious to omens of either triumph or demise, a variety of distinct religious traditions muddle along in every society on the planet, following a trajectory of development, innovation, and continuity that no one has successfully predicted.

While a pantheon of great thinkers failed to pinpoint religion's future, the effort each made to identify the fundamental features of religion refined our understanding of religion as a human experience. Freud taught us how formative childhood experiences can be in the expression of religious longings. Marx taught us how religious organizations and their rhetoric can be wielded by some to the detriment of others. The works of Smith and Smith laid bare the desire for religious unity and harmony frequently hidden under the trappings of a particular religious commitment. My prediction of the jolt cyberspace will have on the future of religion comes with no guarantee that every element will be fulfilled; but it is a venture that can advance our comprehension of the intersection of religion, communication, and community—an incredibly important gain in our information age.

Online Religion and the Future of Religion

Using a computer for online religious activity—an intriguing, albeit marginal, pastime to which interactive computing was put in the late twentieth century—could become the dominant form of religion and religious experience in the next century. If so, religious expression and experience will change dramatically. Each chapter in this book describes an aspect of online religion and then discusses its potential impact on the future of religion. Chapter Two examines the influence of online religion on the horizon of human spirituality. Chapter Three examines its influence on our concepts of time. Chapter Four considers its impact on religious communities. Chapter Five explores online religion and our ideas of good and evil. Chapter Six examines how cyberspace accelerates the closing of the gap between religion and popular culture—a turbo thrust to the rising power of popular religious movements. Chapter Seven looks at how involvement in cyberspace influences human self-understanding, altering people's ability to relate to traditional religious ideas of self and world. Chapter Eight looks at online religion and ideas of the end of time, including the religious extremism historically motivated by this concept.

If current trends in online religion continue, the heavy reliance on image that online religion encourages could lead to a direct competition between religion and mass-mediated entertainment as people seek provocative, inspiring images to anchor their lives. An inherent characteristic of online religion is that its content and presentation are replicable. This simultaneously makes religious diversity uniquely accessible and threatens to undermine the value of the original and unique persons, places, or things associated with religion. Oddly enough, such a combination of factors could reduce interreligious conflict by making faith less linked to and less protective of local roots and particular persons. A different religious future, indeed!

The current era has seen some profound thinking, as well as some overhyped events. Where have we been in the last thousand years? Where will we be at the end of this new millennium? Even a cursory glance at the past makes it clear that human experience has changed markedly from era to era. The ideas we inherited regarding the start of human life have been demolished by technology. Today, reasonable people can no longer agree on a common story about precisely when life begins. As opposed to the largely Christian mores of medieval Europe, which did not consider a fetus a human being until it was "quickened" or "ensouled" by God roughly fifteen weeks into the pregnancy, modern technology penetrates the womb and enables us to imagine life as starting immediately upon conception. Boundaries marking the end of life have shifted as well. People live twice as long as the average person did at the turn of the last millennium; where life ends and death begins is now an ongoing debate rather than a given assumption.

Knowledge has expanded as well. A typical American or European teen knows more history, science, physiology, and math than the best-educated emperor did in the year 1000. We are more aware of others than ever before—not in a modernistic sense, where we see people from other cultures as exotica that spice up our own life (as in the nineteenth century), but in a postmodern sense, whereby people live according to divergent moral, ethical, and aesthetic perspectives.

People are drawn to technologies that fulfill their dreams or allow them to expiate their nightmares.

The Western, liberal view has been to move toward celebrating this complexity, toward understanding the presence of so many "others" on the globe not as threats but as vital resources—of cultural innovation, of entertainment, of medical and philosophical wisdom, of love and beauty. Thus it is not an accident that the online technology that gives diversity its fullest public expression stemmed from a Western, liberal, democratic country. People are drawn to technologies that fulfill their dreams or allow them to expiate their nightmares.

At times, I wonder what Freud might have said about the current state of affairs. After all, he famously described religion as illusion, as a fantasy of wish fulfillment. He urged humanity to turn away from religion, to pay attention to the state of society rather than pray or wish for a father in the sky to take care of things. Would it have surprised Freud to know that religion shows scant sign of abating at the start of the third Christian millennium and that the most sophisticated trappings of modernity in the form of the computer and computer-mediated communications do not provide a haven of escape from religion but instead a popular vehicle of religious practice and religious expression for millions?

To emerge fully, global religions needed a place like cyberspace and a technology like CMC. Now they have both. Cyber-skeptics have responded to the public's fascination with cyberspace and related phenomena by unearthing the gushing predictions of some about the drastic changes the introduction of radio and television would unleash. Though no one ever argues the point very well, the idea behind such rancorous comparisons is to claim: "See? People said the world would be different with radio, movies, and television, but hey—it's just the same old world, isn't it? So why get excited about cyberspace?"

But *is* it the same old world?

Online religion is both a product and a sign of change. It brings with it a tidal wave of new spirituality that may sweep us all up in its path. We are seeing massive waves of new religious practice—Chen Tao in China is a striking example. This individually participatory spirituality is global news, thanks to the Internet and the intricacies of new media. As religion increasingly moves online, cyberspace can be broadly understood as a global public arena where widely dispersed religious practitioners can meet and become known, or understood alternatively, through intranets, as a technological underground railroad that facilitates organizing around the edges of repressive regimes.

Economic factors may contribute to the computer taking on a dominant role in the future of religion. As the population of the earth mounts, land becomes ever more precious and maintenance of civil life an increasingly expensive task. Given the current rate of economic invest-

> Like the Diaspora synagogues of Judaism after the Second Temple, like the cathedrals of medieval Latin Christianity, and like the Bibles of European Protestantism, online religion possesses the capacity to transform the religious alternatives with which it now competes for human attention.

ment in religious buildings, many of which enjoy only limited use, space and economic pressures may make online religion an attractive alternative to the built religious environment. Because in the United States religious groups are given special tax relief, future municipalities may restrict the amount of space they are willing to allot to religious activities; the effect will be to make online religion an attractive alternative for new groups. Efforts to limit or curtail zoning for religious use are already a prevalent feature of urban areas.

Like the Diaspora synagogues of Judaism after the Second Temple, like the cathedrals of medieval Latin Christianity, and like the Bibles of European Protestantism, online religion is a form of new religious practice that possesses the capacity to transform the religious alternatives with which it now competes for human attention. Thus from young to old, from East to West, our religious landscapes could change dramatically in the next decade.

To the extent that past events afford useful insight to what we can expect, the immediate future of faith should consist of more and more online religion that will flourish and diversify. Online religious battles may erupt as established online religions attempt to create and enforce barriers against latecomers and those whose beliefs they consider heterodox. A transformed offline religion may be in the future for faith as well, as people strive to adapt offline religious practices to the tastes and assumptions cultivated by online experience. In real-life worship, look for keyboards in pews, sermons e-mailed to your home account, virtual baptisms, a simulcast *bris.*

Welcome to the spirituality of the third millennium: online religion. Log in. Enter your name and password. . . .

The Ultimate Diaspora: Religion in the Perpetual Present of Cyberspace

Materializing a perpetual present, cyberspace offers the ideal public space for a people without history.

Americans, historian Elliott Gorn maintains, are increasingly "a people without history."

Absent a workable understanding of the past, Americans are "poorly prepared for what is inevitable about life—tragedy, sadness, moral ambiguity"—and "reluctant to engage difficult ethical issues."[1]

The computer craze of the last decades exacerbates Americans' loss of the past. In the electronic universe, history can vanish in a nanosecond. Everything is present. Cyberspace is the now, slicked up with a glittering allure of future presents to come. The shadowlessness of cyberspace, its essential blankness, may explain, in part, Americans' fascination with it. Materializing a perpetual present, cyberspace offers the ideal public space for a people without history.

In the online world, traditional religions such as Judaism and Christianity advance a striking contradiction to this trend. These religions excel in constructing and perpetuating particular memories. They bring to the Web well-honed talents in preserving the past. For traditional religions, a tight relationship exists between normal, face-to-face activities and the content of Websites. In real-life gatherings in homes and synagogues, Jews carry forward in time the story of their ancestors' exodus from Egypt, not once or twice but every year at Pesach. On the Web, Jewish sites bring cherished texts to the electronic medium through online Torah education, Parsha commentaries, "Ask the Rabbi" interactive sites, and even a Cyber-Seder (see Chapter Four).

In churches each Sunday, Christians recount the story of Jesus' life and suffering, his death and resurrection. In cyberspace, Christian Websites typically link to versions of the Bible, display images of Jesus, and present the sponsoring denomination's unique relationship to the central Christian story. Such linkages suggest that although traditional religions are opting to place iconic representatives of themselves in the perpetual present of cyberspace, they do not consider themselves to be of it. They have waded into its churning flow to proclaim that there are some things that do not change.

As a depthless America moves further away from its cultural roots and into the twenty-first century, the need for memory skills becomes increasingly acute. Amid this scarcity of tradition, the memory expertise of traditional religion is extremely valuable. Online religion keeps this expertise just a few keystrokes away. Religious organizations that narrate their stories online imbue the virtual environment with memory-rich claims. The Web pages associated with traditional religions are signposts displaying stories and experiences that their constructors believe must not be left behind, even in cyberspace. These Web pages are a virtual anchor to the past. As such, online religion introduces depth and stability to the virtual environment, perhaps keeping it from floating away into a turbulent future (that is, assuming online religion is not paved over by virtual commerce).

┬ *The Waters of Soul Change* ┴

Our spiritual ethos is as ubiquitous to us as water is to a fish. But like water, its pervasiveness makes it nearly impossible to see. Consequently, we can easily overlook changes in it when they occur, even when they dramatically affect our existence. Amid the shift from the second millennium to the third, a major change began in our spiritual environment, stimulated by the computer and its offshoot of computer-mediated communications. What the final results of this change will be is one of the intriguing religious mysteries of our age.

Although the computer itself is easy to see, the effect that the spread of computers is having on our spiritual environment is not. The influence of the computer begins with its effect on what literary theorist Walter J. Ong, S.J., described as the human "sensorum." Increasing reliance on electronics is transforming the habitual interplay of sound and smell, sight and touch, through which we experience life. It affects our imagination as well. The get-rich stories of Silicon Valley billionaires give evidence to the extent to which cyberspace colors our hopes. Y2K fears revealed how easily the computer can take over our nightmares as well.

These changes are reaching the personal core of each of us, to touch what customarily has been called the human soul. Signs of the soul change that is under way can be found in altered spiritual needs and attitudes, new private dreams and public visions, changed relationships to their bodies and material surroundings, novel emotional palettes and moral sensibilities. Each change is an adaptive response to fluctuations in our spiritual environment, brought about by changes in the basic context of human experience.

All these changes become quite evident in cyberspace. Online religion puts our contemporary spiritual ethos on display, bringing the changes it is producing into view. The effect of the computer and CMC on contemporary religious beliefs and practices is profound and diverse. Much as the printing press sparked a radical transformation of society and culture in the sixteenth century, the computer and CMC are electronically bulldozing the symbolic terrain for religions around the world. Providing the means by which a new set of players can disseminate religious ideas, cyberspace makes a popular transformation of religion more probable. At the same time, it is a vehicle through which religious authorities can promulgate "orthodox" messages into the home of every online follower they can attract.

Computers and Spiritual Change: A Little Background

ENIAC, the first modern computer, was a room-sized machine. Built in the 1940s by IBM, it required specially conditioned air to function and was capable of performing only simple mathematical calculations. By the late 1990s, computers with capacities far exceeding those of ENIAC had no special environmental requirements and could easily fit on a desktop; indeed, there were portable counterparts that fit inside a briefcase.

The rapidly evolving computer was put to fascinating uses, among them communicating with other computers (via a protocol, across telephone lines, through a modem). Begun as a strategic defense initiative by the U.S. Department of Defense, the first computer network, ARPANET (Advanced Research Projects Agency Network), was established in 1969 to constitute an assault-proof communications network for key strategic defense installations. As of the early 1980s, computer communication networks had spread to institutions of higher education and business corporations—and from there well beyond, to the general populace. A major criticism of this expansion was that the general populace that had access to these networks was not truly general but geographically clustered in the first-world industrial and postindustrial nation-states possessing sufficient infrastructure and economic excess to support their development.

Internet is the term used for this world-spanning conglomeration of interconnected computer networks. (A similar but smaller, "stand-alone" set of interconnections, as is found in an office, is known as an *intranet.*) The initial uses of the Internet included electronic mail (e-mail), transfer of files (via a file transfer protocol, or FTP), bulletin boards and newsgroups (Usenet), and remote computer access (via Telnet). In 1989, two graduate students, Tim Burners-Lee and Mark Andreessen, independently devised the idea of the World Wide Web (WWW). It was a globally interconnected set of "pages," readable from any computer in the world that had a software program to access them (known as a Web browser). Within two years, the WWW became the most active aspect of computer-mediated communications.

The term *cyberspace* was introduced by science fiction author William Gibson in his 1984 novel *Neuromancer.*[2] It referred to the partly imaginative, partly concrete experience of place that people have when they are engaged in computer-facilitated electronic communications. At its most basic, cyber-*religion* refers to the presence of religious organizations and religious activities in this semi-imaginary place.

Traditional and alternative religious groups concur that cyberspace is a place where they wish to have a presence; consequently, there are thousands of religious Usenet groups and e-mail discussion lists, intranets, and official Websites. At a typical religious organization's Website, "Web surfers" (as people who explore the WWW are called) can find an introduction to the religion that describes its official history, its major beliefs and rituals, its sacred texts, and a directory of local groups.

As an incredibly diverse collection of religious groups move into cyberspace, one significant effect is the incidence of new convergences and cooperation among them. It is not at all rare for the Website of a Christian group espousing strong millennial beliefs to be linked to a Jewish Zionist Website, for example. Cyberspace has also become a place where a significant amount of popular religious expression transpires. By the late 1990s, it was common for people who had undergone novel religious experiences at large parachurch events such as the "Toronto blessing" to congregate afterward in cyberspace to confirm and support each other.

It also became commonplace for religious groups experiencing considerable tension with society to use the Web to communicate their stance on issues to the wider world. One infamous case involved the alternative religious community Heaven's Gate in Southern California (see Chapter Eight). Shortly after thirty-nine members of the group were found dead on March 25, 1997, it was discovered that Heaven's Gate had posted a farewell statement to the world on its Website.[3]

Another significant consequence of cyber-religion has been the gradual emergence of new, electronically inspired religious practices and ideas. As religious groups grew accustomed to maintaining a presence in cyberspace, they developed innovative uses of CMC for spiritual practices: online global prayer chains, e-prayer wheels, and even online multiuser religious rituals. In a more mundane vein, there was also a plethora of online religious instruction and cyberspace-linked social justice activism.

A provocative development arising from the intersection of cyberspace and religion was the repeated attempts by some to launch pure cyber-religions, that is, religions whose sole existence transpired in cyberspace. To many, these attempts raised problematic questions regarding the value of face-to-face human contact. Equally innovative and no less controversial was the onset of various hybrids, as people associated with traditional religion attempted to relate their faith to and through the new medium. One early innovator was Jacques Gaillot. This Roman Catholic bishop was in regular conflict with the Vatican for his willingness to turn to the media to express disagreement over official Roman Catholic teachings. After using French television to criticize orthodox Catholic positions on such subjects as priestly marriage, Gaillot found himself reassigned from the French diocese of Evreux to that of Partenia—an obscure, largely nonexistent area located somewhere in the Sahara. In response, he established a Partenia Web page (www.partenia.fr) and declared himself bishop of cyberspace, where he ministers to all who contact him in his virtual parish.

Changes in Our Dreams: The Techno Holy Grail

During the medieval era, a desire to locate the cup out of which Jesus drank at the Last Supper—referred to in popular Christian lore as the Holy Grail—swept through the European Christian populace. Stories recounting the whereabouts of the Holy Grail inspired Christian peasants, children, and kings alike to abandon traditional ways of life to pursue the Grail's mystic essence. Today, millions behave as if the computer exudes a comparable aura. They credit cyberspace with salvific potency. The search for the latest and best electronic technologies is altering our world, luring inventors and investors, ideologists and everyday people ever onward in pursuit of some elusive virtual essence. This search is transforming the global economy. It is yielding the richest people in the world.

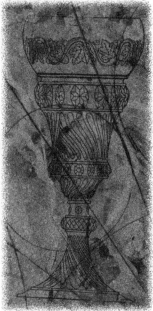

Like the Holy Grail of ancient Christian legend, the Techno Grail of a seamlessly wired life vanishes as anyone draws near it. Modern-day knights who are willing and able to spend endless amounts of money come closest to having it in their grasp. It is possible, they proclaim, to attain a sense of being in the presence of an electronic transcendent. You can download in milliseconds. You can upload in even less. A spectrum of colors and sounds appear at your slightest touch. Lights come on when you speak to them. Whatever you want to know, see, or hear appears in an instant. With access to the exclusive MIT computer laboratories, you can even feel images on a computer screen by way of sensory input accessories called haptic devices.

But given the regularity of technological breakthrough, within a few months our electronic knights realize that the sense of perfection they attained though the technological transcendent was an illusion. The "real" Techno Grail, whose marvelous properties muddy the divide between humanity and machine, between humanity and death, is associated with the next new product. Electronic pets are, at most, a decade away. Haptic sexual encounters are likely even sooner. If computer guru Ray Kurzweil's predictions prove accurate, computing machines will be so complex by 2029 that they will be conscious, their "mental" processes indistinguishable from those of a human being. We have already created machines that can see farther than we can see, move faster than we can move, lift more weight than we can lift. What role will be left for us to play on earth once we invent machines that can think better than we can? Machine maintenance? But the lure of the Techno Grail is so strong that we go on thrashing our way toward it, regardless of the price we—or others—must pay to draw near.

> If the current rate of change holds, the barely imaginable today will be the commonplace of tomorrow. We must get our imaginations in order.

Thinking optimistically, perhaps we will devise computers that mediate human differences so well that they make the politics of oppression and resentment obsolete. If so, we can expect human tyrants to attempt to destroy the machines, while human liberationists risk their lives to save them. All this seems quite implausible now; but if the current rate of change holds, the barely imaginable today will be the commonplace of tomorrow. We must get our imaginations in order.

The Techno Holy Grail, like the Holy Grail of the medieval era, is inspiring its own waves of crusades and crusaders. The first wave, peopled by military personnel working with the new thinking machines, transformed the concept of military preparedness. The ability to communicate uninterruptedly is now a baseline feature of contemporary military initiatives. We expect bombs to be smart and helicopters to be equipped so that the people piloting them can see and hear through walls. Computer-generated battle simulations and computer-monitored missile installations are standard military fare. The dangers and delights this first wave brought with it exploded into popular consciousness through such entertainment vehicles as the 1983 film *War Games*.

Subsequent waves of techno-devotees continue to wash over us. One introduced a substantially reconfigured way of doing business. Retailers advance the idea of the World Wide Web as a perpetually open global mall. The question of what to do with the local malls constructed in the last decades of the twentieth century (thanks to the spread of another all-conquering technology, the automobile) will become an important public policy issue.

Another wave of techno-crusaders is attempting to storm the ivory tower of education. Their goal is to transform our means and methods of instruction by moving it from face-to-face encounters in classrooms to online distance education in cyberspace. Health care, entertainment, banking, and finance have each been refashioned by a computer crusade. Although the focus of this book is on religion and the Internet, it is not only religion that the Internet is profoundly changing .

Humor and Religion: The Froth on the Wave

In *The Name of the Rose*, Umberto Eco used a murder mystery as a window onto religion and the intellect in the medieval (Latin) West. In Eco's tale, a scholastic effort to synthesize Greek philosophy and Christian tradition at a medieval monastery is halted when the ruling abbot comes across a manuscript by Aristotle praising the value of humor. The abbot is confronted with a genuine dilemma. What should he do when the monks endeavor to prove the universality and omnipotence of God by showing how divine revelations occur in non-Christian texts leads to evidence that might undermine the value of seriousness itself? Eco's abbot suppresses the Aristotelian paean to humor both by concealing its existence and by poisoning the corners of the pages of the manuscript so that any reader wetting a finger to turn a page will die. This ploy yields a trail of dead monks who eventually provide sufficient evidence for the mystery to be unraveled by a visiting priest.

Eco's fictional abbot would be appalled were he to encounter online religion, where farce and sacred freely intertwine. The Web pages of online religion routinely jest with forgiveness, with confession, with sin, with love, with the very idea of God. On a Web page that proclaims itself to be "God's home page," God is presented as an elderly, white, male cartoon character. Drawn with a Ziggy-like body, God wears a loose white robe and sports long white hair, a long white beard, and a halo. He greets those who log on to his page with the words:

Hi there. I'm God. How are you?
Get out of my way!
I am God and this is my homepage.
I am the creator of Life, the Universe, and everything. However, I am not responsible for Micro$oft Windows, your slow bandwidth, and Netscape's BLINK tag.

HTTP://WWW.NETSTORE.DE/~GOD/

So God may be the creator of the universe; but with fine, dry humor this cyber-author dons the persona of God to assert that when it comes to the virtual elements of cyberspace (computers and software), all theological bets are off.

A cybernetically frustrated God with a biting attitude might be sufficient to send Eco's abbot screaming back to the Middle Ages. An encounter with a few of the repentance Web pages sprinkled throughout the WWW would surely do so. Dozens of them offer blank windows in which prospective virtual penitents are invited to describe the deeds or thoughts they regret and then click on a button underneath the box. When they do so, their confessed transgression is immediately wiped out, vanished, gone. It brings new meaning to the phrase "wiping the slate clean."

Although humor is, of course, not present on every Website with religious or spiritual content, it is remarkably prevalent. The anonymity integral to cyber-faith encourages the impish nature of fledgling virtual theologians. Does this mean that online religion is necessarily sacrilegious? Does the widespread use of puns, cartoons, funny sound effects, and the like mean that cyber-faiths are incapable of summoning the majestic in its religious aspects?

Apparently not. Just as a Website displaying a punning cartoon God may be a feature of cyberspace, one also finds breathtaking sites of classical religious art (www.vatican.va), sites that enable visitors to practice online transcendental meditation, Bible teaching and research Websites, and so on. In other words, though humor is a feature of many religious Websites, religious seriousness is also widely prevalent.

The religious humor of cyberspace is the froth on the wave of religious change. No longer is religious humor something of the back door, the alleyway, and the basement. Cyberspace makes religious humor just as public as religious seriousness. This is a unique development in religion. To the extent religions have wrestled out for themselves a respectable public cultural role, they also sought to relegate punsters who wished to jest with their symbolic goods to private, back-of-the-house spaces at best or to the dungeons or gallows at worst. But in cyberspace, religious humor is an escapable part of the wave.

Technology and Faith

Faith and technology can seem totally unrelated topics, but their influence on each other is substantial. Religion speaks to humanity most powerfully and authoritatively at the limits of human control over daily life. Technology extends the boundaries of human control; thus the operating arena of religion is diminished. In earlier historical periods, if someone came down with a high fever and purplish blotches all over the body, a shaman was requested to intervene in the realm of the spirits. Today, a typical response would be to drive to a local doctor's office or hospital for treatment—or go on the Internet to investigate symptoms and possible treatments.

Religion, which specializes in actions and ideas at the boundaries of human sovereignty, is finding its symbolic goods veering into obsolescence, thanks to technological advances. At the same time, new technologies, which necessarily create new areas of the unknown in their wake, open up previously unforeseen realms of religious need. Hence technology necessitates development of new rituals, theological meditations in a different vein—attempts to forge a new equilibrium of human attitudes and behaviors, toward an ever-shifting unknown, building viable bridges to the divine.

Because the relationship between technology and faith has been well tracked by scholars, I am free in this book to concentrate on the specific interactions of religion, spirituality, and computer-mediated communications. For those interested in a general exploration of technology and religion, I recommend David F. Noble's *Religion of Technology* and Frederick Ferre's *Hellfire and Lightning Rods.*[4] These wonderfully rich, easily accessible works are a great starting point for those who wish to investigate the relationship between technology and faith.

From Orality to Scroll to Codex to Secondary Orality to Hypertext

The changes set off in religion by the transition from oral-based to scroll-based cultures were immense. For oral cultures, rhetoric (or the "technological" organization of verbal communication) was a crucial art. Human memory was of paramount value. Passing along historical experiences, rituals, and ideas about the divine in story form was more conducive to maintaining capacities. Humanity's religious impulse was expressed in oral stories and public rites, each passed on, in essence, by a guild of experts to apprentices who then shared them with the community as a cultural heritage.

With the move to writing and scrolls, the value of certain types of human memory receded. It was no longer necessary to be able to recount from memory lengthy narrative passages seamed together by commonly known metaphors. With the move to scrolls, one had to master symbol systems, alphabets, words. Yet the structures of oral memory influenced the earliest move into writing and scrolls. What was recorded on them was entered without gaps between words or sentences, without capitalization or punctuation. Oral memory was still required to make sense of the written text; therefore, orality remained the dominant paradigm for historical knowledge. Scrolls were, initially, a method by which oral memory was supplemented and aided.

Scrolls had scant influence on the popular imagination. For the masses, cathedrals and temples, home rituals and community festivals were for centuries the dominant bases of religious understanding and practice.

There were serious mechanical limitations to scroll documentation. Only one portion of a scroll could be accessed at a time. Indexes were an impossibility. Scrolls did not store easily. Since it was not easy to change the content of a scroll, scroll-based texts tended to be revered as completed or perfect objects. The limitations of scrolls meant they had scant influence on the popular imagination. For the masses, cathedrals and temples, home rituals and community festivals were for centuries the dominant bases of religious understanding and practice.

But the ascendancy of the scroll was advancing. The shape of human memory that soon became most valued was simultaneous familiarity with oral traditions and comfort with symbol systems. One also needed to recall where things were. For religion, the move into writing and producing scrolls led to formation of canons—bodies of knowledge that defined the tradition authoritatively. Interestingly, the move to written authority staked out new perimeters for the priestly caste while subtly setting the stage for its undoing. Symbol decipherment was a skill that could be learned. Thus, at least hypothetically, the knowledge of religious authorities became more accessible, no longer the property right of a particular family, class, tribe, or kin line.

The move from scrolls (handwritten information recorded on a continuous sheet, rolled up and stored) to codices (sheets of paper printed using movable type, with the individual sheets bound together) changed religion once again. In contrast to the hand-crafted scroll, a codex could be easily and massively reproduced, thanks to the printing press and movable type. The size of a scroll was finite; a codex was assembled sheet by sheet, meaning it was well adapted to extended works. Just as vitally, the sheet format enabled readers to move back and forth among its disparate parts with ease. Indexing became possible as well, so that one could include with the codex a key to its contents.

The effect on religion of the move to codices was immense. Eventually, it led to pamphlets and books, which overtook art, architecture, and ritual in informing the popular religious imagination. Early in its introduction, the codex had a radicalizing effect. A fifteenth-century Bible scholar named Martin Luther understood the potential of movable type and exploited the new technology to wage the first print propaganda campaign against the prevailing religious authorities of his day.[5]

The next major change in the means of historical memory that had a material impact on the nature of religion was television and video recording. We are almost too close to this change to see it accurately, but it is characterized by the slow ascendancy of image over word, with retinal stimulation valued more than cognitive content. The effects of this development on religion are still taking form. Worship services are designed to look like television events, with their messages crafted into a series of information packets, each timed to last about as long as snippets of television programming squeezed between commercials.

The move into "hypertext"—online text and images interconnected via Web links—set off by the development of the World Wide Web is in this regard a serious matter. Will it erode traditional means of religious authority or alter even further our common patterns of worship? Online religion may be the activity where the cultural impact of hypertext first becomes evident.

If the Virtual Is Sacred, What Is the Profane?

Online religion has dedicated fans. Many online religionists readily express avid enthusiasm for the inspirational contributions cyberspace has made to their spiritual life. They see the Web, the Internet, the entire phenomenon of computer-mediated communication as a tremendous advance in human solidarity and oneness. Christian theologian Jennifer Cobb claims that in building these communicative technologies, we have merely hardwired our preexisting interconnectedness. Cobb contends that in cyberspace, we have externally actualized our evolving psycho-spiritual ties with one another.[6] It is a fascinating, if unprovable, theory.

Some paeans to cyberspace read like a delightful romp in a playground. With gleeful, utopian schmaltz, the anonymous author of the following poem, which made the rounds of cyberspace in a multitude of versions, used a child's voice and the custom of a child's bedtime prayer to articulate delight in online connections. Note the subtlety of the theological argument inserted in the middle of the prayer. It offers a justification that God should bless the computer because the ability to form and maintain online relationships is analogous to the ability to form and maintain a meaningful relationship with God.

My Little 'Puter Prayer

> Every night I lie in bed,
> This little prayer goes through my head:
> May God bless my mom and dad
> And bless my children too.

And God, there's just one more thing
I wish that you would do.
If you don't mind me asking,
Would you bless my 'puter too?

Now I know that it's not normal
To bless a small machine,
But listen just a second
And I'll try to explain.
You see, this little metal box
Holds more than odds and ends.
Inside those small compartments
Rest a hundred loving friends.

Some, it's true, I've never seen,
And most I've never met.
We've never even shaken hands
Or truly hugged, and yet
I know for sure they love me
By the kindness that they give,
And this little scrap of metal
Is how I get to where they live.

By faith is how I know them,
Much the same as you,
And sharing our lives brings them close—
From that our friendship grew.
Please take an extra minute
From your duties up above
To bless this little hunk of steel
That's filled with so much love.

A prayer to God to bless one's computer is, by extension, a prayer to
God to bless cyberspace. The bountiful presence of online religion testifies

to the fact that, for millions, this imaginative domain is already enfolded into the sacred.

If computing machines are deemed sacred—are aspects of our material world that people pray over and for and through—what does this imply for the boundaries between the sacred and the profane? This is an especially perplexing dilemma, if we take into account that the computing machine (on which a child prays for God to bestow a blessing) is technically immediate kin to computing systems that monitor nuclear warheads, manage stock exchanges, and run water processing plants. It raises the question of whether it is really the computer per se that the poet wishes God to bless, or rather any element of the world that makes greater human connection and interaction possible. To the extent the latter is true, homage paid to the computer may be a new-millennium acknowledgment of our vital need for attachments to each other and our willingness to welcome anyone or thing that facilitates our ability to be social.

Though online traditional religion gives cyberspace a much-needed link to the past, its very presence online is likely to reconfigure religions nonetheless. It is not that these religions could overtailor their message to suit the medium; already deeply involved in cyberspace, they show scant signs of doing that. Rather, a by-product of participating in the medium could be substantive change. Consider a handful of illustrations:

⌘ Making religious texts infinitely accessible and malleable, cyberspace undermines the numinous quality of sacred writings.

⌘ A grassroots, participatory medium, cyberspace makes it possible to bypass the formal hierarchies that predominate in religious circles.

⌘ A fantasy universe that stimulates the imagination but ignores the rest of the body, cyberspace is a nonenvironment that sucks attention away from the immediate surroundings in which most traditional religious life occurs.

⌘ A cool medium that rewards pithy phrases, cyberspace makes unwieldy the extended reflection on the transcendent that religion requires.

⌘ An oversaturated information place, cyberspace adapts best to specialized, niche knowledge distinctly at odds with the integrated wisdom that religion promotes.

Each by-product eerily confirms the insight of Marshall McLuhan (a true techno-prophet): for the information society, the medium is the message.

Conclusion

As with the earlier influential shifts in the human spiritual landscape (such as the Protestant revolution in Christianity), online religion is a popular social movement as well as a social product of cultural elites. Global religious organizations have established an official presence in cyberspace, planting the flag of faith just as explorers of old staked out the terrain for themselves.

Thanks to the limitless electronic terrain of cyberspace, right next to such bona fide cyber-religious presences (and possibly with just as impressive an appearance) may be raucous religious satire or a freewheeling spiritualist offering neomystic Tarot readings. In cyberspace, online religion resembles nothing so much as an electronic *souk* of the soul.

Examining the evolution of online religion in cyberspace gives some intimation of the direction human spirituality may take in the third millennium. Some people already navigate the virtual world with grace and ease; others are hard at work constructing their first virtual surfboard. Whether you choose to surf or run, the tidal wave of computer-inspired spiritual change is coming. Though the particular variations in religion it will unleash are unpredictable and at this point extremely difficult to perceive, you can no longer say that you weren't warned.

The flowering of online religion is an amazing feat. An unfathomable amount of volunteer labor and human creativity was required to build the cathedrals and synagogues of cyberspace that already exist. The imaginative energy of this new medium is fueling a new dimension in religious practice and thought. Rushing toward us, online religion crashes against the shoals of more traditional religious ideas and practice. Sometimes it is pushed back by the encounter, but like the tidal wave it is, sometimes it overwhelms them—and anything else in its path.

As cyberspace swiftly overtakes us, we can no longer choose to avoid the change it brings. Instead we must determine how best to respond. Given that outrunning a tidal wave is never an option, the best possibility open to us may be to run *toward* the wave, to leap into its force and surf its energies to a new shore. If so, we may find that surfing spiritual change is exhilarating, frightening, and slightly dangerous. It may even be fun. Regardless, in this case it is a necessary skill, given our techno-cultural circumstances. A tidal wave of the spirit is already upon us, though few realize it.

In cyberspace, online religion resembles nothing so much as an electronic "souk" of the soul.

A Taste of Forever: Cyberspace as Sacred Time

Online, it is possible to feel you have lived and loved a lifetime in a day.

Time. Fixed in our imaginations as an absolute, time is lived relatively. An autumn hour whiled away in lively conversation with an intimate friend concludes in an instant. A summer hour spent standing in line at a stifling branch office of the Department of Motor Vehicles passes like congealed molasses. To those deeply engaged with it, cyberspace transmits a multiple sense of time. It forcefully expands time, subtly serving up distinct experiences of timelessness (as those who pay for an Internet service provider at an hourly rate can attest). It freezes time, causing everything to exist in a perpetual present. In cyberspace, Usenet conversations from a year ago are statically preserved in virtual amber, intact as the instant they were posted. Cyberspace also powerfully compresses time. It is not uncommon for a virtual acquaintance met a few weeks ago to seem like an old friend. Online, it really is possible to feel you have lived and loved a lifetime in a day.

Together, these divergent streams constitute the unique phenomenon of cyber-time. At once an idea of time and a complex set of time experiences, cyber-time establishes the daily horizon along which millions live. Since it is possible to log on and access the virtual cosmos from anywhere, cyber-time can make the entire world seem orderly, neat, intelligible. An explosion of computers has placed cyber-time in effect in offices and homes around the world. Data organizers, cell phones, and other new digital technologies place it on, and soon within, our bodies. Increasingly, cyber-time sets the rhythm of life for people far outside the confines of its specific audience. It informs the experience and sense of what time is for the world at large. It fixes the parameters of work and rest. It influences our assumption about what constitutes the past. It molds our ability to conceive of the future.

A potent attraction of world religions is the unusual experience of time they deliver.

Since the third millennium is apparently to be an age dominated by global consumer capitalism, it is not surprising that our dominant idea of time stems from the era's consummate consumer product: the computer. Cyber-time is a key psychological underpinning of modern consciousness that is scantily acknowledged. Yet its import was flushed into everyone's view for a moment when the Y2K computer glitch loomed near. Immediately after the year 2000 arrived *sans* large-scale computer collapse, the fuller implications of the Y2K near-panic were allowed to slip silently into the abyss. The brief glimpse of our global dependence on the electronic environment was evidently too threatening to pursue.

Whether cyberspace merits the primary role it has come to occupy in organizing our lives is to some extent a subjective decision; however, since cyberspace has quickly grown central to our time sense, much work needs to be done if we are to have any say in its temporal influence—unless, of course, we prefer to march to the beat of a virtual drummer we scarcely know or understand.

A potent attraction of world religions is the unusual experience of time they deliver. Walk into St. Peter's cathedral at the Vatican, the great Hindu temple of Madras, or the Shinto forest in the heart of downtown Tokyo, and you can feel time shift, regardless of your religious orientation. The reaction is no accident. Religious leaders, architects, and artisans

Give Me That Online Religion

have conspired for centuries to produce such an effect. It is wryly amusing to realize that cyberspace—not online religion specifically, but cyberspace in general—accomplishes almost accidentally the psychological time shifting that artists such as Leonardo da Vinci labored for years to achieve. Cyberspace is sacred time. It imaginatively endows those who encounter it with alternative time experiences.

The interrelationship among people's experience of time, time regulation, and religion is not new with cyberspace, but in cyberspace, the relationships occur in a novel form. In previous cultural eras, religion led the way in developing and inculcating ideas of time. Religious people kept track of time to regularize prayer or worship. Whether accidentally or intentionally, their timekeeping habits spread into wider society and organized social life. In cyberspace, the opposite is true. Commercial interests push cyberspace as a remorseless time regulator. For a small but growing segment of the populace, cyberspace imposes a nonstop pace on daily life. With neither sun nor moon to rise or set, the virtual horizon of cyberspace teems with activity, twenty-four hours a day, seven days a week, fifty-two weeks a year.

If online religions bore the same temporal relationship to the nonreligious organizations that share their environment as real-life religions typically have to those who share theirs, online religions would stand out as locales of time difference. Like a meditation prayer room in an airport, online religion could offer a valuable respite from a perpetually hectic environment. But for the most part it does not. Much of online religion exhibits the commercial aesthetic that infiltrates the rest of cyberspace. Rather than provide a singular antidote to the ceaseless undulation of virtual-commerce time, online religion mimics the restless pace of e-commerce. It, too, is open "twenty-four, seven." To keep Websites going, online religionists stock their sites with banner ads and push religious products. As a result, it can be difficult to distinguish them from commercial sites. It is enough to make one long for a special, subsidized ".re" domain for which only nonprofit religious organizations and spiritual communities qualify.

†Religion, Time, and Technology: From Praying Monks to Cyberspace⨼

The biblical religions that are the backbone of Western culture—Judaism, Christianity, and Islam—uphold a dual concept of time. For human beings, time is an unfolding straight line. Unidirectional, purposeful, and limited, it furnishes the stage on which God interacts with humanity. Human time was launched from the bow of God at Creation, according to orthodox biblical tradition. Winging through space like an arrow, it ends when it hits the target of final judgment and salvation.

The second idea of time that orthodox biblical religion supports is godly or sacred time. Nondirectional and limitless, sacred time is eternity, the essential temporality of the divine. A concept that theologians even today struggle to explain, eternity as a dimension of the sacred consists of all times at once. As in the concluding scenes of Stanley Kubrick's movie classic *2001: A Space Odyssey*, where the surviving astronaut, Dave, is a young man encountering himself as an old man encountering himself as a baby, sacred time is substantively omnitemporal. It is time folded upon itself, completely available from any point, time as an aspect of existence that occurs without boundaries.

In the Euro-American West, blame or praise for our propensity to account the passage of time precisely and honor it as an axial factor in social life can partly be laid at the feet of ancient Christian monks. In accordance with biblical tradition, Christian cenobites (community monastics) believed that a heavenly time also existed. It was different from time on earth. Where earthly time caused everything to change—to break up, decay, and die—heavenly time was a magical elixir. Those who sipped its nectar endured forever.

Longing for heaven and desiring to taste its timelessness on earth, desert monastics organized time so they could live as if they were already there. They invented a pattern of life that revolved around orderly spiritual practice. Dividing each day into eight intervals, or hours, they arranged their activities around recurrent communal prayer services that accorded with each interval. Seasoning earthly time with what they believed was divine atemporal flavor, the monks created an approximation of heaven on earth for themselves, as least as far as time was concerned.

Practical challenges confronted the monks who undertook to realize this ideal. To gather communally at regularized intervals eight times a day required technology that could ascertain when the intervals occurred, as well as means to notify the monks as each interval drew near. The notifying technology the monks developed was simple. It consisted of ringing bells. Simple as it was, the technolo- 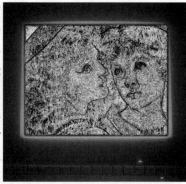 gy had a profound effect. Because it was impossible to constrain the sound of pealing monks' bells to the confines of a monastic compound, they resounded over the countryside. Gradually they became the rhythmic standard for wider communal activity as well.

Monastic timekeeping is one minor example of how the biblical religions have contributed notably to our understanding of time. Ideas of time are applied to regulate human life. Technology is the means by which regulation is accomplished. Religions often inspired the effort. In the case of the ancient monks, an idea of time generated correlating practices and sparked interest in sympathetic technologies. However, ideas of time do not necessarily come first. Sometimes a technology is developed that makes certain ideas of time realizable. Such is the case with cyberspace. Although not intended as a time-regulating device, the technology of cyberspace has had impressive temporal aftereffects. Most critically, harking back to the ancient monks, cyberspace breathes new life into the sacred idea of eternity.

Cyber-Eternity

Shared human spaces are the arenas in which competing concepts of time and their regulating technologies contend with each other. As a globally shared space, cyberspace might have been a pivotal site where concepts of time, religious or otherwise, contested for prominence. Instead, the supporting technologies of cyberspace imaginatively accord with a particular metaphysic of time: omnitemporality, the religious idea of eternity as perpetual persistence. Given that the initial flowering of computer technology occurred in the West, computer users' cultural history assuredly contributes to this "reading" of cyberspace by its inhabitants. People customarily relate to emergent technologies by means of practices and ideas with which they are already familiar. For time, the idea of eternity was readily at hand, bequeathed through ancient Jewish and Christian beliefs. It is interesting that a cultural bias influenced the choice of the reigning interpretive lens used to make sense of cyberspace, but this does not negate its effect.

Continuously accessible and ostensibly disconnected from the cycles of the earth, cyberspace appeared to its first Western consumers to be a concrete expression or materialization of the monks' concept of eternity. They christened it thus. It is always present. Whatever exists within it never decays. Whatever is expressed in cyberspace, as long as it remains in cyberspace, is perpetually expressed. According to recurrent Website testimonies, the quasi-mystical appeal that cyberspace exudes stems from this taste of eternity that it imparts to those who interact with it. But it is not just any slice of eternity that cyberspace serves up. It has introduced its own unique cyber-eternity to the world. At least, this is the concept of time that people interacting regularly with cyberspace often credit it with having.

That cyberspace is taken for a materialized instance of eternity may explain in part our passionate obsession with it. This may also account in part for our incessant willingness to invest an immense proportion of global resources into its continuously morphing hardware and software. To the true believers, cyberspace is temporal heaven. Except, of course, it isn't. There are delays, downtimes, crashes. There are limits imposed by hardware and software. There are viruses, bugs, and glitches. When myriad people attempt to access the same site at the same time, you may find yourself surfing cyberspace at a pace that makes a hundred-year-old turtle's waddle look speedy.

On the Web, few are willing to acknowledge the intrusion of temporal realities into the dream of cyber-eternity; but those who do often have a sense of humor. They design Web pages that poke gentle fun at what insiders call the World Wide Wait. Seven Flags Over cyberspace is one such site. Its welcome page opens with a large, square photo of abandoned cars in a dump. With their doors askew, frayed seats, and opened hoods revealing the void where an engine should be, the cars are a visual metaphor for promise versus the occasional reality of cyberspace. The authors playfully compare cyberspace to amusement parks. Like them, cyberspace promises a utopian experience that it cannot always readily supply:

Welcome To Seven Flags Over Cyberspace. We hope you enjoy your visit. You are currently in the parking lot waiting for one of our rapid shuttles to whisk you away to the various amusements. Unfortunately at this time many of the rides and exhibits are unfinished, owing to a small number of piddling labor disputes and certain minor technical problems. Be that as it may be, there is still plenty of fun just waiting for visitors to enjoy.

HTTP://HOME1.GTE.NET/LAFRANKS/INDEX.HTM

Employing an image-based comedic riff that endeavors to make waiting in cyberspace as amusing as Disney tries to make standing in line for the

Pirates of the Caribbean, the Seven Flags authors propose that if you are forced to wait in cyberspace, you should relax. Have fun. Look around.

Other sites ignore the temporal shortcomings of cyberspace and instead laud it as a credible instantiation of eternity. To these people, cyberspace is a place whose temporal dimension, whose *when,* is unlimited. Hence they believe that cyberspace is a site where matters of eternal significance can and should be expressed.

Cyberheaven is a paramount example of a site whose creators treat cyberspace as a hub of eternity. The Website is a virtual cemetery, where people memorialize deceased loved ones. Cyberheaven's authors expressly describe the site as a place analogous to heaven. It is, they insist, a place where time is eternal. Against a background of clouds and a picture of a female angel standing behind and guarding two young children, the site's introduction makes the eternal qualities of Cyberheaven clear:

This is a memorial to pay homage to our love ones and friends. A special place in cyberspace to insure the preservation of all their memories. A memorial that will live on in cyberspace for eternity. This is a visual memorial that can be visited at any time and from any place world wide. This allows you the opportunity to visit your Love Ones any time you like.

HTTP://WWW.TEEMAX.COM/**HEARTS**.HTM

Twelve names are listed in the Cyberheaven index. Its links take visitors to individual Web pages that display a photo and a brief tribute to the person who died. Their messages call poignant attention to lost love, and the authors' wish that through the Website, the love they feel will endure eternally. These homages to the deceased, eternally lodged in Cyberheaven, are profoundly moving; but there are not a lot of them. Evidently, when it comes to one of the most serious time-related issues, that of finitude or death, cyberspace has not yet been adjudged a trustworthy instance of eternity.

The elusive tang of cyber-eternity is a recurrent theme in countless online conversations. Web pages are dedicated to musing about its eternal character. In one site, cyber-author Wendy M. Pfeiffer expounded on the attributes of cyberspace's unique brand of eternity. Her central thesis was that the concept of time that cyberspace promotes is distinct from time as experienced in lived, face-to-face interactions because it is grounded in digital technology:

I wonder if the things we know about time apply in cyberspace? There's an immediacy to actual space that is missing in the electronic universe. Perhaps immediacy is the wrong word. The Internet and e-mail and computers are supposed to save time, to shorten cycles, to speed collaboration. Yet they don't force the immediacy present in the most innocent conversation. This medium travels faster than my thought processes. At least once a week I send an e-mail that I later regret. The undertow of thought, which might have lessened the effect of the first wave, always travels more slowly than that first, mighty swell. Yet, that undertow is present in tandem when I'm speaking face to face. Since I believe the rate of my thought processes to be relatively predictable, I have to assume that time is somehow affected differently between the two spaces.[1]

A fledgling virtual sociologist as well as a cyber-philosopher, Pfeiffer compared the shortened time expectations of computer-mediated communications to those of other electronic products. Each claims to expand the time in our lives by shortening the time required for everyday maintenance activities such as cooking. Emotionally, these products transform human impatience from a shortcoming to be corrected into a need that must be satisfied:

There's probably a corollary here to microwave time. Sixty seconds spent heating a cup of hot water in a microwave do indeed last an eternity compared to that first minute just after you hit the snooze alarm. Is cyberspace uniformly related to time, or does time ebb and flow in relation to cyberspace like it does in relation to the physical realm?[2]

Formidable as its influence can be, technology is not the only thing that sways the human experience of time. Pfeiffer ponders the varying experiences of time that human life itself serves up in moments of tragedy or despair:

I remember a night in Dallas several years ago. On that night, I was choosing between life and death. The space in which the decision was playing out—my mind—was as disconnected from the physical as cyberspace. That is, there were some fitful connections from time to time, but they were dynamic. I was wandering through mental space at a fantastic rate, using and discarding resources, a branch here, a bound there. At one moment, I was a frightened six year old and an old woman, alone and bitter. And I discovered, in that moment, a truth about space and time: they are anchored in our relationships and experiences. . . . Why, then, do the rules appear to change in cyberspace? Is cyberspace really "space" at all, or is it simply another view of time? Can we ever escape this physical space while our relationships anchor us?[3]

To Pfeiffer, cyberspace is less a place than a *when* achieved by technology. Where we are, who we are with, and what is going on between us constitute our experience of time, and cyberspace provides them all.

Y2K: The Technological Tribulation

Public response to the potential computer glitch known as Y2K was minimal at first. It was hard to grasp why the fact that early generations of computers were programmed to recognize two digits representing years, rather than four, should be a major cause for concern. But as time progressed, an incipient Y2K panic flared, and the illusion of cyber-eternity was acutely disturbed. In 1998 and accelerating into 1999, popular rhetoric contended that computers were about to fling us into global disruption. Y2K was a mouse that would roar around the world. National leaders expressed shock as they were told about the havoc that computers programmed to recognize only the last two digits of a year's date might wreak on their populations.

The United States led other nations in publicizing and addressing Y2K, but even America did not have the mouse completely captured by 1999. According to the January 1999 quarterly assessment of the President's Council on Year 2000 Conversion, American businesses needed to develop contingency plans laying out what they would do if the computer environment collapsed:

What once was a rational decision—to use two digits to represent the year in many computer systems—is now the Year 2000 (Y2K) problem, an enormous challenge to governments and businesses around the world. . . . At the Federal level, agencies are working to prepare critical systems for the Year 2000, and have mounted aggressive efforts to ensure that critical services will not be disrupted by the transition to the new millennium. . . . There is still time remaining for organizations, especially smaller firms, to prepare their critical systems for the Year 2000 . . . all organizations should be developing back-up, or contingency, plans to address internal and external Y2K-related failures.

HTTP://WWW.Y2K.GOV/NEW/FINAL2.HTM

Since Y2K prophets believed the computer glitch was going to set off a debacle of horrifying proportions, the impetus among them was to warn the populace of the impending peril. When computer engineer Ed Yourdon announced on a discussion list that he was going to pull his elaborate Y2K site in mid-1999, he received a passionate plea from Kurt Semler not to take his information off the Web:

Just remember this, on the day you close your website, you are depriving 5,000,000,000,000 people of your valuable information. Please reconsider the closing of your website. PLEASE!!!!

HTTP://GENERAL.FORUMS.COMMENTARY.NET/FORUMS

Across the World Wide Web, a trend to interpret Y2K through the lens of divine judgment ran rampant, with Protestant Christians leading the way. Some equated cyberspace with the Tower of Babel. In a Web post by the

Rev. Jerry Falwell, cyberspace was referred to as a "tower unto heaven." Falwell claimed that just as in the biblical story of Babel, the goal toward which humankind directed its technical prowess had gotten it into trouble:

As the world prepares to crash into the 21st Century, with all the predicted crises and catastrophes which may begin happening at 12:01 am on January 1, 2000, we must remember that a similar international event occurred long ago. It occurred when the masses decided to circumvent God's plan of salvation and build a tower into Heaven.

HTTP://WWW.TRBC.ORG/MEDIA/SERMONTEXTS/980830.HTML

The fact that this text was posted on the Web (attached to the walls of Babel?) introduces an ironic humor to his protest, which Falwell evidently misses.

A second biblical parallel that cyber-prophets employed to describe Y2K was to depict it as an element of the Tribulation, the period of strife, civil war, and global chaos that Christian premillennialists associate with the end of history (see Chapter Eight). Fundamentalist pastors such as Jack Van Impe preached that Y2K fulfilled biblical prophecy and was a "sign of the end times." Van Impe was so convinced this was the case that he and his wife, Rexella, made a video titled *2000 Time Bomb* that they marketed on the Web. The ad copy on the Web describing the eighty-minute video used stark, premillennialist language and images to describe Y2K:

The so-called "millenium [*sic*] bug" could scramble the electronic minds of computers worldwide in the year 2000 . . . and the universal panic inspired could be the catalyst for the rise of the antichrist, the mark of the beast "666" system[4] for buying and selling, and the advent of the great tribulation! See how the effects of this predicted computer catastrophe coincide with Bible prophecy regarding the coming of the Lord and the latter days of time on this earth! Will you be ready to protect your home, family, career, savings and future? This powerful video prepares you for the coming chaos and offers hope for the future.

HTTP://WWW.JVIM.COM/CATALOG/I2000TBV.HTML

Though he refrained from mentioning Y2K by name, Falwell was a leader among those who interpreted Y2K as an end-times phenomenon:

In fulfillment of Bible prophecy, the world today is beginning to speak the same language. We have become an urban society with nearly six billion persons mostly living in large cities. We are satellite and Internet connected. We are fast moving toward a cashless economy . . . a one world government . . . court . . . and a one world church. We are building a universal city with a one world church whose tower reaches into heaven. But, the Trinity has come down and looked us over. And it seems that God doesn't like what He sees. He may be preparing to confound our language, to jam our communications, scatter our efforts and judge us for our sin and rebellion against His lordship. We are hearing from many sources that January 1, 2000 will be a fateful day in the history of the world. And, as brilliant and scientifically advanced as we are, it all slipped up on us without fanfare and in the most simplistic manner.

HTTP://WWW.TRBC.ORG/MEDIA/SERMONTEXTS/980830.HTML

Not all online Christian evangelical voices were quite so pessimistic. Some evangelical Christians considered the potential catastrophe of Y2K an excellent opportunity to demonstrate the communal value of their beliefs. These technological Noahs built cyber-arks of information and resources that they hoped would carry society through any technology deluge. Many moderate online evangelicals used the Web to publish information about potential Y2K problems and encourage people to do what they could to minimize Y2K risks to themselves and others. A parachurch evangelical Christian media enterprise, the Christian Broadcasting Network (CBN), used television, books, and videos along with cyberspace to disseminate Y2K warnings, each carefully anchored in a biblical passage. Their main recommendation was that people stay calm but be prepared. They recommended, among other preparations, obtaining copies of important financial records; stockpiling goods and supplies; and preparing to do without heat, water, or electricity for an extended period.[5]

The Joseph Project was another such effort. According to its Website, the sole intent of the project was to minimize the impact of Y2K on global populations, as a testament to their faith:

> The Joseph Project 2000, a Christian-led nonprofit, seeks to prevent and respond to the potential impacts of the Year 2000 computer problem in a biblically balanced and professional manner, honoring and glorifying God in all we do.
>
> HTTP://WWW.JOSEPHPROJECT2000.ORG/

Though Joseph 2000 was clearly on the bandwagon of the Web as cyber-ark, its founder, evangelical Christian Bill Bright, also believed that Y2K was an excellent opportunity for evangelism:

> We realize there are many other issues to consider, such as how to prepare and serve our staff members (especially those ministering overseas) where Y2K problems may be much worse. Therefore, we are supplying information and web links through which they can obtain information to evaluate the problem where they minister and make their own decisions. We are also taking steps to ensure that electronic fund transfers proceed with minimal problems. Having said that, we realize that the psychological issues may outweigh the technical. Americans used to living fifty years in a society with few potential nationwide disasters may feel a great deal of anxiety leading up to January 1, 2000. Therefore, we seek secondly to bolster the faith of believers and thirdly to compassionately witness to nonbelievers.
>
> HTTP://WWW.JOSEPHPROJECT2000.ORG/BILLBRIGHT.HTML

A Website titled God's Wilderness was representative of the extreme pessimism at the other end of the spectrum of religious responses to Y2K. Presuming that Y2K would be a catalyst for world disaster, the beginning of a technological tribulation that would make urban life unlivable, these Y2K pessimists fled the cities and established technology-proof living compounds in the American backcountry. But how could a small, obscure, poorly funded group of individuals inform others of their decision to forsake contemporary technology—much less urge interested parties to join them—except by extending an invitation via cyberspace? Even the most extreme Y2K technophobes came up with no satisfactory alternative to the Web, so they published the news of their intention to break with technosociety by way of the global bulletin board:

After many years of living in the northwoods, and after most of our children were "up and out" we felt led of the LORD to sell some of the God's Wilderness land. We just wanted to sell bare land. Because there were all ready other Christian families in the area we simply placed a small add in World Magazine asking for "Christian Home-schooling families to purchase Northern Wilderness land." When interested people began to look at the land they informed us about Y2K. . . . We have no desire to commercialize on Y2K. It takes more than just a desire to relocate, more than even the money to do it. We believe the most important factor is that families KNOW that the LORD is leading them to make the move.

HTTP://WWW.LAKENET.COM/~DWHNJH/HELPAG~9.HTML

The film *Titanic* became a mega-hit as the Y2K crisis gathered steam. But instead of being a straightforward reprise of the disastrous sinking of the technologically dazzling ocean liner, the Y2K saga was an inversion of it. In the film, after the ship rammed an iceberg, news that the "unsinkable" *Titanic* was going down was restricted to a few, while everyone on board could see that the ship was sinking. In the case of Y2K, warnings reverberated throughout cyberspace and the nonvirtual world that the computer environment was about to crash, while everyone saw that things continued to work.

On December 31, 1999, and January 1, 2000, there was scarcely a computer gurgle. Faster than the hula hoop, Y2K was declared passé, and the year 2000 was labeled a nonevent. Perhaps that is why, post-*Titanic*, ship travel never regained its cultural prominence, while post-Y2K the world silently reembraced cyber-eternity. As for the prophets who had barked out warnings that cyber-eternity was over, with nary an apology they began to bray about other signs of the end times.

Uploading as Eternal Life

The illusion of timelessness in cyberspace tempts some cyber-travelers into longing to meld with it. These cyber-mystics dream of leaving their bodies behind to become one with the Net. There are Web pages where people online debate the desirability of uploading as an experience of eternal life. In an "R. U. Sirius" interview with Rudy Rucker, a professor of math and computer science at San Jose State University and a prolific author widely proclaimed to be the founder of "cyberpunk science fiction," Rucker described the possibilities he saw for uploading, as well as some of its apparent shortcomings. (In the title of the interview, note the term *fleshware,* which calls attention to the bodied ground of the virtually published exchange.)

FLESHWARE: AN INTERVIEW WITH RUDY RUCKER

R. U. SIRIUS: What do you think about Carnegie-Mellon Roboticist Hans Moravek's notion of people actually uploading their consciousness into the Net?

RUCKER: I'm into it, in a way. It's a complicated question and I've thought about it alot for many years. It was sort of the idea in [the novel] *Software* that the robots were going to get this man's personality. You would first need a database. You would need to be interrogated over a long period of time. . . . It would generate this hypertext file. It might be called a lifebox. You'd give it to your grandchildren and they can say "Did you ever play baseball grandpa?" and it would tell them. And they could say. "Tell me more," and so on. It will be a hypertext memoir. If it's done well enough you can actually talk to the person. Of course, just because you write your memoir, the book isn't you. You're dead. The question is, how good would the simulation have to be for you to feel like it was you?

SIRIUS: Or can you give it a conscious experience?

RUCKER: If a robot is complicated enough, maybe it would feel like it was conscious.

HTTP://WWW.INTREPID.NET/~MAGMEDIA/PREVOLTING/FLESHWARE.HTML

The designers of this page, however, want to make money as well as promote their belief in uploading. To read the rest of the piece, viewers are required to send $25 to the author. You can explore uploading as eternal life, but only at a price.

Promoting the idea of the transhuman (of which the cyborg is one instance; see Chapter Seven), some Web authors contend that uploading is the equivalent of eternal life (though not the sole path to it). Uploading is merely one means being investigated alongside various other bio-genetic undertakings that are part of the dream to transfigure human existence.

Intriguingly, the dream of uploading as a form of eternal life does not appear explicitly on religious Websites. It is instead the religious dream of eternal life rendered in the worldview and language of science and philosophy; consequently, it shows up on pages dedicated to speculative science and cultural futures.

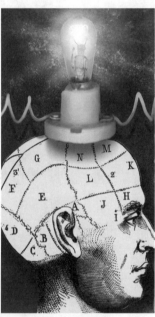

One is the Transhuman Web, a collection of links to sites dealing with the next phase of human existence. One link is to a page containing arguments in favor of both downloading and uploading as viable means to achieve eternal life. Nick Bostrom, in the Department of Philosophy, Logic, and Scientific Method of the London School of Economics, opines that uploading the synaptic matrix of one's brain would make backup copies of the self permanently available for downloading and thus offer the means of achieving perpetual existence. Yet, he contends, it may also be possible to skip the back-and-forth procedures and upload directly into the Net:

If we could scan the synaptic matrix of a human brain and simulate it on a computer then it would be possible for us to migrate from our biological embodiments to a purely digital substrate (given certain philosophical assumptions about the nature of consciousness and personal identity). By making sure we always had back-up copies, we might then enjoy effectively unlimited life-spans. . . .

HTTP://WWW.HEDWEB.COM/NICKB/TRANSHUMANISM.HTM

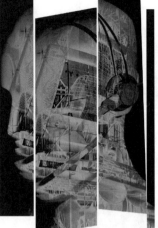

Uploading into cyberspace as a mode of eternal life attracts artists as well. The pioneer artist-visionary of cyberspace was Gibson, whose *Neuromancer* introduced the term *cyberspace* to the world and gave us the premier depiction of the process of mentally jacking into the Net. Self-proclaimed transhumanist artist James William Lewis argues on his Website that there is little to prize about the human bodily condition and its "meat brain." He opens the site with a graphic in the upper-right-hand corner of the welcome page, which proclaims that computers will equal humans in 2016. For Lewis, whose goal is to become one with the computer, it cannot happen soon enough:

A Transhumanist Artist realizes that Extropy will enhance human abilities to sense, perceive and manipulate the cosmos. We know that in a gigahertz world, our sluggish, 100 cycle/second brains are too slow, are virtually blind, are unable to directly transmit their contents to other meat brains, and die about the time they have been fully educated. Being trapped in a meat brain is a cruel fate for any human consciousness. But that will all change soon. Children born in 1998 will see human equivalency before they graduate from high school. If they choose to transfer their consciousness, they will be the first generation to never die. They will also be the last generation of biological humans.

HTTP://WWW.CYBERLEWIS.COM/GRAPHIC/POSTHUMAN/ARTTALKA.HTM

To Lewis, creative people play an important role in the transition of humanity to a postbiological state. They will formulate the aesthetic and cognitive horizon necessary for the changeover.

Artists and Philosophers have a big, tough job starting now. Using our slow meat brains, we must somehow envision the minds of transhumans operating thousands, perhaps millions of times faster than biological brains. . . . The first persons to cross over may initially become disconcerted, terrified or suicidally depressed. Suddenly, they will have perfect memory. . . . Biological humans will seem incredibly stupid and useless. What will be the meaning of "self" and "someone else?" of "here" and "there?" "then" and "now?"

HTTP://WWW.CYBERLEWIS.COM/GRAPHIC/POSTHUMAN/ARTTALKA.HTM

Though Lewis is willing to discuss his role as a transhumanistic artist with anyone, he does not flame or fight about it. To him, living eternally entails a new social ethic where we all really must get along, since no one is ever going away:

I will discuss any transhumanist topic with anyone. We will agree to be nice in our discussions because we are going to live forever and we don't want to feud with each other for the next thousand years.

HTTP://WWW.CYBERLEWIS.COM/GRAPHIC/POSTHUMAN/ARTTALKA.HTM

Whether scientists or artists, would-be uploaders espouse a new utopian religion. They have seen their city on a hill. It is one whose rhythmic pattern is the sacred time of cyberspace eternity. It is one that has no bodies in it. They sail toward cyber-eternity with passion and fervor, despite infrastructure shortages and the likes of the next Y2K panic. They are the millennial pioneers of cyberspace.

Escaping the Dominance of Cyber-Time

Like the pealing of monastic bells, the reverberations of cyberspace time travel far outside the boundaries of any virtual community. They further a horizon of historical imagination where action is instant performance. As we become acculturated to the speed of the virtual universe, our patience with each other and with our nonvirtual material environment shrinks. An expectation of immediacy is widespread. To satisfy it, even more technologies are being developed. We expect instant accessibility to people and have designed cell phones and pagers to achieve it. We expect instant accessibility to knowledge and have devised twenty-four-hour-a-day news channels to provide it. We expect instant availability of products and have designed retail operating systems that keep stores continuously open to offer them.

Cyberspace time further whittles away at human patience by nudging a concrete society into a pattern of activity devoid of sleep cycles. This may be stimulating for the short run, but it simply is not sustainable as a long-term pattern for human living. To people awash in finitude and flaws, to people who require episodes of rest and quiet, cyberspace eternity—no matter how attractive—has an almost punitive character. Since the concept of eternity first arose in religious circles, it would be an odd historical reversal, then, were online religion to distance itself from the eternal characteristics of cyberspace to emphasize the daily nature of ordinary life. Yet this is precisely the religious palliative painfully absent from the virtual landscape.

Cyberspace time further whittles away at human patience by nudging a concrete society into a pattern of activity devoid of sleep cycles.

Cyber-Seekers: Stories of Virtual Pilgrimage

Give me that online religion,

give me that online religion,

give me that online religion,

it's good enough for me. . . .

No evidence indicates that any extant religious group includes "Give Me That Online Religion" as part of its sacred music repertoire. But as hymn writers compose lyrics that reflect contemporary religious experience, the verse could soon be sounding from congregational settings in the next few years. Online religion is a consequential spiritual practice for a sizable portion of the cyberspace population, a group whose size increases exponentially month by month.

Individuals with no tie to any particular religious organization or group are the pioneers of online religion. These nonspecialists find in cyberspace a public space where they can preach and teach, crack religious jokes, and construct virtual rites with abandon. And they love it. To computer-adept amateur religionists, the global interconnectedness and pervasive openness of cyberspace concoct a heady brew of spiritual possibility that causes the spiritual imagination to flourish. Investing hundreds of hours in constructing Websites filled with spiritual content that they treat as virtual sacred places, individual online religious practitioners are the cultural missionaries of virtuality. They are among the first to explore the boundaries of cyberspace, attempt to learn its language, and try to translate their religious message into its context. Netcasting virtual religious art and music, these cyber-religionists construct online rituals, spin out virtual theologies, and form unprecedented, free-floating bonds of spiritual community in an eruption of cyberspace spiritual enthusiasm.

People involved with new and alternative religions have rapidly followed those pioneering spiritual virtuosos into cyberspace, contributing to the plethora of religion online. Reflecting the marginalized status of their traditions, they design Websites in an apologetic mode, using them to explain to the "outside" world that they pose no threat.

In cyberspace, pastors and priests, rabbis and imams diligently strive to translate or interpret the historic messages of their tradition into virtual geography and digital sacred time.

Although they became active in cyberspace much later than the pioneering individual religionists and the marginalized traditions, mainstream world religions are vigorous participants in online religiosity. This includes major religious institutions (such as the Vatican, www.vatican.va) as well as some that can take a Web surfer by surprise (the Amish, www.800padutch.com/askamish.html). In cyberspace, pastors and priests, rabbis and imams diligently strive to translate or interpret the historic messages of their tradition into virtual geography and digital sacred time.

The Websites of traditional religions typically present an introduction to their beliefs, a directory of congregation locations, a calendar explaining upcoming religious events, and a prayer room. Other Websites, explicitly labeled "unofficial," exist for many religious traditions, too; they are maintained by followers for whom the site is a vehicle to argue on the Web with the hierarchy of the traditionalists, organize lay support for the tradition's initiatives, or express their enthusiasm for or disgust with the religionists in charge.

Thus today, virtual home sites for online religion are being constructed by practically every religious group with active adherents. Yet the vast majority of people involved with online religion are not those who build the amazing textual and image edifices of virtual spirituality. Instead, they are those who come to inhabit them. They are people who find or seek out online religion, valuing it because it meets a pressing spiritual need. In the semi-imaginative locale of cyberspace, accountants, factory workers, lawyers, students, and assorted others do not just trade stocks, participate in eBay auctions, and view scanned risqué photos. A sizable percentage have novel religious experiences.

Cyber-Pilgrim Tales

The versatility of online religion becomes clear when we examine people's interactions with it in detail. As we follow Ashley's participation in a Jewish Cyber-Seder, David's visit to an online Benedictine monastery in the New Mexico desert, and Julia's use of the Internet as a medium for neopagan magical practice, we gain a reasonable appreciation for the spectrum of lived religion in cyberspace.

Commonalities

Although the stories of Ashley, David, and Julia represent too small a sample to warrant generalization about online religious practice, their commonalities and differences offer rich clues to a viable direction for future research. The commonalities are principally demographic. Like most of the people who currently use the Net, Ashley, David, and Julia are English-speaking, college-educated people of Euro-American descent. They also either have sufficient disposable income to pay for private Internet access or are engaged in activities that make access available to them. Limitations in civic infrastructure or Internet availability were not a problem for any of the three.

Differences

The differences among their stories span a wider range. Diverse motives inspired Ashley, David, and Julia to become involved with online religion. Ashley was prompted by a romantic relationship with someone of another faith. David got involved with online religion when he plunged into Web surfing to distract himself from the aftermath of a divorce. For Julia, the Internet itself was the primary attraction; she wanted to explore the boundaries of its spiritual possibilities.

Another way in which the stories differ is the extent to which each person perceived online religion as a form of religious novelty. For Julia, online religion was a distinctly new spiritual activity that cyberspace made possible. For Ashley and David, online religion simply provided novel access to a traditional religious practice. Though the online religious activities in which these two engaged were new to them, neither Ashley nor David perceived online religion as an encounter with religious innovation; on the contrary, they claim it helped them connect to "old-time religion," and their subsequent behavior supports that claim.

Online religion offers a distinct instance of human spirituality that is valid in itself.

A third difference is the validity of online religion that each credits. To Ashley and David, online religion functioned as a sign; it pointed to but did not contain sacred meaning. Through online religion, they connected with what to them were valuable transcendent goods, but they soon left online religion behind for face-to-face religious congregations and tangible sacred texts. By contrast, cyberspace for Julia was and is a singular sacred dimension. To her, online religion offers a distinct instance of human spirituality that is valid in itself.

Ashley and the Cyber-Seder: Interreligious Love

Growing up in a midwestern, middle-class family of Irish-English descent, Ashley regularly attended her neighborhood Presbyterian church from the time she was born, without giving it much thought. Obtaining a degree in nursing from a local college and starting work at one of the two hospitals in her hometown, she continued her involvement with the same small congregation where her parents had taken her as a child, again without giving it much thought.

Shortly after turning twenty-five, Ashley met and began dating Michael. A doctor on staff at the hospital where she worked, he was an observant Jew. Religion was rarely a topic of conversation between them until about a year after their first date, when they began discussing marriage and the possibility of having children. This led to serious conversations about religion. Michael told Ashley he was willing to consider becoming a Christian, but she was reluctant to urge him to do so since he had been far more involved in his religion than she was in hers. Before they made any major decisions, she said, she wanted to know more about Judaism. But she preferred to learn about it on her own rather than simply through Michael.

An avid Internet surfer, Ashley chose to begin learning about Judaism by logging on to the Internet. She went to Yahoo.com and typed "Judaism" into the main search box. Aimlessly scrolling down the links that were retrieved, she found information for potential converts, Torah classes, Hebrew instruction, a "virtual Jerusalem," and even a Website that offered to have any message she would write placed on the Western Wall (www.aish.com/walcam/).

But the link that intrigued her the most extended an invitation to attend a Cyber-Seder in a few weeks' time. She noted the date on her calendar and resumed searching online for a connection with Judaism that had thus far seemed elusive.

In Ashley's case, it took a multimedia effort to get her involved with online religion. Although she had learned about the Cyber-Seder online, she claims the only reason she ended up participating in it was because of a National Public Radio segment. In a series of daily national announcements, the local NPR affiliate station broadcast a short piece promoting the online Cyber-Seder. Hearing it, Ashley recalled the Website she had found and decided it offered the means by which she could participate in her first Jewish ritual. So she chose to begin her exploration of Judaism by participating in a Cyber-Seder.

At the Cyber-Seder Website, Ashley learned that this was the third year for the Cyber-Seder, frequently described as the largest seder in the world thanks to its composition of onsite and virtual celebrants. Organized by the Knitting Factory, a company dedicated to bringing new Jewish music traditions to the world, the event was a third-night seder that took place IRL (in real life) at 7:30 P.M. on April 12, 1998, at Lincoln Center, New York. The event was simulcast on the World Wide Web at www.jewmu.com/cyberseder/.

In Hebrew, *seder* means "order." The text read aloud and discussed at a seder is the Haggadah, which draws on the Bible, Talmud, and Midrash writings to tell the story of the Jews' exodus from Egypt; it thereby fulfills a command of the Torah to recount the exodus story. According to Michael Dorf, who organized and led the Cyber-Seder feast, more than three thousand editions of the Haggadah have been used in Jewish tradition. The Cyber-Seder Haggadah incorporated poetry by Allen Ginsberg, violin music by Laurie Anderson, a reading by Lou Reed, and a *shofar* and clarinet duet, along with customary biblical and Talmudic passages. This eclecticism reflected the combination of self- and other-directedness of this unique religious event.

In an online introduction to the Cyber-Seder, Dorf explained that the planners intended it to be a celebration involving more than solely Jews:

This evening we will knit the sections of the Haggadah with performances from many gifted artists. Freedom of expression is to be open, outspoken, challenging convention, and finding inspiration to address the realities of the time and imagining how to change it. This clearly transcends Judaism and links all people.

Ashley had thoroughly investigated the Cyber-Seder Website a day earlier, which turned out to be a useful investment of her time. Two special software plug-ins were necessary to participate in the Cyber-Seder. (Plug-ins are software programs that automatically integrate into and extend the

In the folkways of virtual conversation, chat room names are adornments, Christo-like fragments of textual landscaping attached to one's prose as an intentionally constructed part of the communicative exchange.

software platform on a computer.) From links provided at the main Website, Ashley downloaded and executed the prerequisite plug-ins in less than five minutes—free of charge. Consequently, on the day of the Cyber-Seder, she merely had to show up at the Website, log in, and click on one icon to launch the simulcast video and sound and another icon to launch the chat room.

"Hi Sarah! Happy *Pesach*!" Ashley was warmly greeted the instant she logged into the chat room of the Cyber-Seder, using the name Sarah. No one in the chat room that evening assumed that was her real name. In the folkways of virtual conversation, chat room names are adornments, Christo-like fragments of textual landscaping attached to one's prose as an intentionally constructed part of the communicative exchange. They are expected to be descriptive, playful, expressive, perplexing. They are not expected to be "real." To attend the Cyber-Seder, Ashley had decided to garb her prose in the name Sarah, after the beautiful, laughing wife of Abraham from the biblical book of Genesis. It presented her accurately as female and was chosen to convey her attitude of openness to the novel experience ahead.

As the crowd for the Cyber-Seder gathered, a wave of anticipation swept over Ashley. At Lincoln Center, where the physical Seder was being held, two cameras were set up in the main hall. They gave virtual participants alternating views of the main stage and those gathered in the main hall and simultaneously fed, to all those logged on, live sound from the hall. Long before the Cyber-Seder began, online participants could hear bits of the murmured conversation among those assembling, accompanied by the pleas of Michael Dorf for the more than 650 attending the IRL seder at Lincoln Center to be seated so that the ceremony could start.

Before the Cyber-Seder began, virtual and IRL participants kibitzed about the position of the cameras, gave advice to the regularly arriving newbies on how to get their plug-ins working, and commiserated with those who could not. In one of the ironies of the new medium, California participants were never able to access the sound part of the live feed, whereas Israelis, Canadians, and countless others around the world all had excellent reception.

As the Cyber-Seder started, online participants began wondering whether those connected via the Internet should be considered participants or merely viewers. The question was submitted by chat room participants to the online moderator, who sent it on to Dorf. Midway through the seder, Dorf announced the question to the crowd at Lincoln Center. His answer revealed how much on the cusp of religious experience the Cyber-Seder was: Dorf's answer was, "We don't know."

Long portions of the Cyber-Seder ceremony were richly steeped in ancient Jewish tradition, such as hiding the *afikomen* (the middle *matza* of three used in the ritual feast). Although less readily intelligible to non-Jews such as Ashley, these gave virtual attendees some exposure to the main elements of a conventional seder celebration. An interreligious flavor was added when the Knitting Factory showed a video of the Rev. Dr. Martin Luther King Jr. giving his "I Have a Dream" speech midway through the seder. An effort to universalize the seder was also made by one speaker who psychologized the story. He declared that the underlying message of the seder story is for each of us to come out of our internal enslavements, that people must fight to free themselves from the tyrants within that bind them.

For virtual participants, a highlight of the Cyber-Seder was the chat room. Many logged in hours before the seder itself started. For the entire time the Cyber-Seder site was active, virtual participants exchanged non-stop messages with each other, as well as with a number of those present in the hall who wanted to interact with the virtual attendees and communicated with them by means of a bank of computer terminals at Lincoln Center.

The Cyber-Seder chat room was a place of great humor and warmth. Virtual participants wrote jokes and then chuckled "out loud" in response to them by typing textual codes such as "LOL" (for "laughing out loud") or "ROTFL" ("rolling on the floor laughing"). These ceaseless exchanges were like the conversations that flow through a crowd at any large human gathering. Ashley found it impossible to understand several entries drafted by chat room participants who, when they wanted to emphasize a particular point, switched to Hebrew. Paradoxically, this pushed participants who did not know Hebrew out of the exchange precisely at the time when attendees frequently were most passionately trying to communicate.

Occasional criticisms of the Cyber-Seder arose online. Traditionally, the seder is a home-based Jewish ceremony that emphasizes family and community closeness. To some, conducting a seder in cyberspace, where people viewed the storytelling in the company of machines rather than one another, was a profound contradiction of the human sociability the seder was dedicated to cultivating. To Ashley, these criticisms were moot. Had there not been a Cyber-Seder, she would have attended no seder at all.

This situation, of interest in a new religion inspired by affection for another person, has a long history in human relations. In one of the most poignant passages in the Hebrew Bible, Ruth speaks to her mother-in-law, Naomi, about her willingness to adopt Naomi's journey, her homeland, her people, and even her God to stay with her:

Wherever you go, I shall go,
wherever you live, I shall live.
Your people will be my people,
and your God will be my God.
Where you die, I shall die
and there I shall be buried.

RUTH 1:16B

Ruth's poignant utterance affirms how love can move people to embrace the values and obligations of someone they love, including their religious commitments. For Ashley, the Cyber-Seder offered a threshold of introduction to Judaism that she could step across. It helped her appreciate the historic values of Judaism that shaped and informed Michael's life. Six months after her Cyber-Seder experience, Ashley decided to convert to Judaism.

Christ in the Desert Monastery: Online Monks and the Spiritual Center They Manage

Having delayed the decision to marry until his late twenties, David did not anticipate getting divorced as he turned fifty. But it happened. Now his ex-wife lived a mile away. The two shared joint custody of their two children, Caitlin, age fifteen, and Peter, age thirteen. The children alternated stays with them weekly. An offshoot of this Solomonic arrangement was that David's life was a never-ending seesaw of chaos and stillness. When the children were with him, he never had enough time. When the children were with his ex, he had more time than he could bear.

A landscape architect who worked out of his home, David began surfing the Net at night during the weeks when his children were away. He started by exploring architecture- and landscape-related sites, but he soon found that his landscaping interests were sated by the time he quit working, around 7:00 or 8:00 P.M. After that, he checked out chat rooms, but none held his interest very long. As conversational playgrounds, chat rooms were not the right place for a tired, confused fifty-year-old.

One evening, David decided to unwind from a long day bent over his drafting board by randomly visiting Websites generated by a wheel-of-fortune Webcaster. The minute he landed at the Christ in the Desert Web page, he was hooked.

The site was an early venture into cyberspace for the Benedictines, a monastic order of the Roman Catholic tradition. It opened with a warm, mustard yellow welcome page, decorated with a watercolor of the

monastery's chapel. Handwritten letters scrambled along the right side of the chapel drawing, giving the page a strong resemblance to an illuminated medieval manuscript. In a variety of typefaces and languages, the Christ in the Desert homepage proclaimed: "Welcome to the monastery of Christ in the Desert." The welcome page gave the day's date and explained its significance for the Christian calendar. David was enchanted. Unexpectedly, the site began to function as a time machine, propelling him back to the catechism classes of his childhood. Though his parents were not practicing Catholics, he had attended Catholic school through the fifth grade and taken the classes necessary to prepare for first communion. He participated in it, but after that, nothing. He did not feel compelled to follow through with confirmation, and his parents did not press him about it.

Surveying the Christ in the Desert site, David found it presented a diverse menu of choices. He could check out "Today's Martyrology," introduced with a one-paragraph mini-hagiography. He could visit the monastery gift shop, where books, music, icons, santos, and potpourri could be ordered. He could, according to the page, seek God by following a link that played online monastic chants. The same link offered information on how to determine whether one had a monastic vocation, how to request prayers, how to learn more about the monks currently in residence, the week's homily, or how to learn more about the retreat house. He could also follow a link that featured a drawing of a monk's head, garbed in a habit, and titled simply "The Porter."

This was the link David chose to follow. Clicking on the monk icon called up general information about guest housing at Christ in the Desert, along with an online form to reserve space there. As he scrolled through this information, David was increasingly intrigued by the idea of Catholic monks advertising on the Web. He tried to imagine what they must be like; but his imagination failed him.

He turned to mulling over the ramifications of his unexpected singleness. What would he do during the summer that lay ahead, when his children would be away at camp a good part of the time? Could a monastery visit be the solution? Spontaneously, he decided it was. He posted a request to visit the monastery for one week in June, noting to himself that he would have to follow it up with a written request and deposit.

David then continued to explore the Website. Two other options were offered on the main menu. One was monastic studies. Following this link, he read about the history of the Benedictine order, about the holy rule that the Benedictines had followed since the time of Saint Benedict in the sixth century. He read a summary of what monastic life entailed, and he scanned the martyr list for the year. Before logging off, he clicked on the final option on the main menu: "Monastic News." There he read excerpts from the abbot's notebook and learned that a new building was under construction at the monastery site. Before shutting down his system for the night, David closed out his Web browser, went into a word processing program, and composed his official letter requesting monastery housing. The next morning, he folded the letter around his deposit check and sent them off by mail. Though the monk who invited him had been virtual, David was about to embark on a real-life religious pilgrimage.

Visiting the Monks

June came sooner than seemed possible.

As David immediately grasped upon arrival at the Website, Christ in the Desert is not just a virtual monastic site. It is an actual monastic community that expresses itself dual-dimensionally. People can visit the virtual Christ in the Desert in cyberspace (http://www.christdesert.org), or they can visit the IRL Christ in the Desert in the stark terrain of northern New Mexico, about ten miles north of Abiquiu (famous as the final home of the painter Georgia O'Keeffe).

David had begun with a visit to the virtual Christ in the Desert only to realize that it was not enough. He followed up his cyberspace visit with a trip to the earth-bound community hidden away in the New Mexican desert, the famous monastery that was home to the monks who designed the Vatican's Web page.

The trip by car from western Texas to northern New Mexico seemed to David to parallel his present situation. On the journey as in his life, there were moments when he was traveling unknown terrain, not sure he was headed in the right direction. His response to each was the same. As a divorced father, David was not always sure how to interact with his children; but he kept trying to be a good parent anyway. On the journey to Christ in the Desert, he kept going as well, even after he lost his way for the fourth time. In either case, it was not hope that kept him going but just basic trust. In the midst of ambiguity, he relied on his instincts—and in geography and parenting, so far they had delivered.

After two days of driving, now within twenty miles of the monastery location, David suddenly was not confident that the turn he made off the main highway onto a red clay road leading out into the desert was the right one. There was no sign or road marker. Still, he kept going, five, ten, fifteen miles into the desert on the deeply rutted, one-lane road. He decided that if it was a wrong turn, he could always spend the night in his car, get up in the morning, and turn around or else keep going till he found the place. Just as he was about to give up and begin scanning the roadside for a turnoff place to park and spend the night, the clay road made a sharp left curve, and he was there.

The monastery buildings blended so perfectly into the desert that they looked as if they emerged from the ground rather than being built on it. In a way, they did. The scattering of low-slung one- and two-story buildings of the monastic compound were constructed of local stone quarried from the desert floor and trimmed in aged, unvarnished wood. A small guest shop and welcome center were located at the front of the site off to the left. Behind them, the two-story guest housing formed a large rectangle, with an open courtyard in the middle. The chapel, the monks' housing, the monastery library, and the monks' work center were all several hundred yards deeper into the desert, accessible from the guest lodges via two narrow, winding dirt paths.

David registered at the welcome center, where he was given a copy of the rules for guests. There was no electricity in any of the cottages. There were oil lamps for light, but no other "modern" comforts were allowed. Talking among guests was discouraged, except on Sunday afternoons in a social room set aside for conversation. It was strictly forbidden

Inside the small, circular stone chapel, Gregorian chants echoed off the walls and circled around the worshipers like the soft cloak of heaven.

to talk during the communal meals that guests took with the monks. Instead, everyone present was expected to listen attentively to liturgies.

At Christ in the Desert, the complete divine office of eight worship services a day was celebrated in old-rite Latin. Morning, noon, and night, bells rang at regular intervals, summoning the community to worship. The pealing kept God constantly on the brain—which was of course the intent. Inside the small, circular stone chapel where each service was held, Gregorian chants echoed off the walls and circled around the worshipers like the soft cloak of heaven.

David recorded his thoughts:

How great to write by lamp light, to see mountains shadowed in dusk, to be away from the daily world. I want to luxuriate in the stillness, to open myself up to the wonder and wisdom of God.

What does it mean to be a Catholic? Does it matter what it means? Or is it more important for me to determine what I as a Catholic should do rather than what I essentially am?

How do I speak about my renewed interest in faith to my children without making them cringe? How do I explain my faith after the divorce? I came here with more spiritual questions than I realized. A chance to meet cyber-monks consciously drew me here, but I also want to sort out the quandaries of my soul. This is a place where a person can find answers.

Walking back to my car after checking into my room, I thought about the name the monks gave this place. Christ in the Desert. Is this desert a place where one can meet Christ? For Christ's sake even more than mine, I hope so. I hope he is here. It is so beautiful—stark and silent and beautiful. What better place could Christ be [in]?

David spent seven days at the monastery. Though he learned that these were the monks who designed the Vatican's Web page, he never saw them at work on Web design. (The monk primarily responsible for designing the Vatican site was visiting friends in nearby Santa Fe.) Halfway through his visit, David asked one of the monks why, given their remote location, they specialized in electronics-dependent work. The monk described the order's choice of employment as a commonplace decision: "All Benedictines have to work to support the order. Many groups bake and sell bread or cookies. Our order opted to go into Web design. This allowed us to capitalize on the skills many of the men joining the order brought with them."

But Christ in the Desert monastery is located deep in the desert, far from any viable electrical power source. Thus the monks' occupational choice presented difficult challenges—particularly regarding how to obtain sufficient power. Ultimately, the monks opted to power their high-tech undertaking with solar panels that took advantage of the natural high-intensity sunlight of the desert locale.

I find myself settling into the rhythms of monastic life more easily than I'd imagined. My plan was to write an explosion of letters and postcards after I arrived; yet, now, I savor the quietness of this place. I wanted to be detached from others for awhile. I didn't realize how strong the wish was till I found a telephone message from an East Coast client tacked to the door of my room. I had not been gone a day when the long, elastic strings of my profession tried to pull me back. In the center of the guest-lodging courtyard, there is a statue of Christ. It is about four feet tall, and has been roughly hewn out of wood that looked like it came from the desert ground. I wonder if a former guest made it? A single red rose blooms in the garden circle in front of the statue, nature's offering to the once-for-all sacrifice. . . .

At the end of the week, David headed back to Texas. He felt renewed, composed, and peaceful. He was ready to jump back into his hectic, disheveled weekly routine. To sustain this feeling of inner peace, he vowed to himself that he would attend mass regularly. He would encourage his children to accompany him if they wished; but he was going to go regardless.

Yet the insights into his own soul were not accompanied by any genuine understanding of the monks. David remained unsure why the perpetually quiet Benedictines, who lived radically separate from the world, were involved in Web design. Had he known a few things about medieval Christian monasticism and the involvement of religious orders in manuscript reproduction, David might have realized that working with texts and icons—albeit electronic ones—was a reprise of an ancient spiritual discipline for monks, as well as a means to secure the income necessary to keep their monastery afloat. But even with this familiarity with the history of Catholic orders, had David pressed the monks to speak about the historical significance of their unusual fundraising activity, he would have learned little. Monks who hail the world in cyberspace do not talk much when you go to see them.

A Witch in Cyberspace: The Internet as a Neopagan Tool

Twenty-eight years old, single, and in her second year of graduate school studying for a Ph.D. in sociology at the University of Southern California, Julia introduced herself to her classmates as a "nonpracticing neopagan," a member of the contemporary Goddess-based spirituality movement whose followers are known for their effort to reclaim earth and harvest-cycle rituals condemned as "pagan" by early Christian officials. It was a memorable introduction, but not exactly accurate. Julia was in fact a practicing neopagan; however, she no longer met face to face with a coven (a kind of quorum of thirteen) or participated in the communal solstice rituals held in forests in the area. Instead, she had opted to be on the cutting edge of a new phenomenon. She was a practicing cyber-witch.

Her involvement in cyberspace neopaganism flowed naturally out of her two principal interests: Goddess spirituality and computers. Her religious history was not particularly unusual. Midway through grade school, her family abandoned all traditional religious practice. With the exception of a heavily decorated fir tree that reigned over the family room for two weeks in late December and an intrafamily exchange of presents after lunch every December twenty-fifth, her mother's staunch Catholicism and her father's moderate Episcopalianism vanished from their lives.

Only Julia retained an interest in matters of the spirit. Seeking an outlet for her interest, she dabbled in Goddess worship throughout high school. Initially, Julia's parents questioned her closely about her involvement with the neopagan crowd, but after they read the literature she brought home and met some of her neopagan friends, they relaxed. Her mother even helped Julia cast a protection spell one day and surprised them both by the keen pleasure she took in the ritual process.

Julia felt that she was participating in a revolution of the human soul.

Julia liked neopaganism's celebration of femaleness. She also appreciated the fact that its liturgies and rites cherished the cycles of the planets. The neopagan community transformed a nearby recreation center into a pagan coffeehouse on alternate Saturday nights. Julia enjoyed hanging out at the coffeehouse; her favorite activity was listening to the Celtic musicians who regularly appeared there.

During the last two years of high school, Julia helped produce and distribute a local neopagan newsletter that announced the places and times of weekly coven meetings, when and where open solstice rituals would take place, and which musicians and artists were in town. It also kept track of neopagan persecutions, reporting when neopagans were arrested or their rituals were disrupted by people who considered such activities heretical or blasphemous. Each time she read a persecution report, her commitment to neopaganism increased. Dismayed that people would respond so negatively to a movement whose goal was reclaiming the joyful play of human spirituality for everyone, Julia felt that she was participating in a revolution of the human soul.

By the time she left for college, her zeal for neopagan practice had waned. Emergent spiritual movements took a toll. Covens were hard to keep together. There were too few people to organize and oversee any activity they planned. Julia also was disturbed that the neopagan movement was becoming heavily commodified. Dream catchers were sold at Wal-Mart. Tarot cards and crystals were available at the town drugstore. Why nonpagans thought it was possible to purchase material goods that would generate spirituality, Julia did not know; but the trend left her uncomfortable.

Computers began to fill Julia's free time. Attending California State University, Long Beach, as an undergraduate, she spent most of her first year in a computer lab doing the online research projects required for class. During those long sessions on the Web, she began reacting to cyberspace as if it were a technological sacred forest. Nestled in mystery, it seemed to her imbued with sacred qualities that made unique magical connections possible.

Julia signed on to a Usenet discussion group whose main topic was neopagan practices. She posted a note to the group, telling them of her spiritual track record. In return, Julia received e-mail that made her realize that a motley crew of neopagans had reacted to cyberspace in almost the exact same way. Some were specializing in developing rituals for a virtual environment. Their goal was to revise customary neopagan rituals to satisfy the constraints and freedoms integral to the online environment. Others were devising mystical games to be played on the borderlands of the virtual and material worlds.

Julia learned of a clearinghouse for cyber-neopagan activity, a listserv named TIAMAT-L (Testing the Internet as a Magical Tool). The plain welcome page of the TIAMAT Website, almost without graphics, offered a neopagan rationale for involvement in online religion along with guidelines for how to translate neopagan land-based rituals into cyberspace virtual ones:

Cyberspace is a unique place to hold a ritual. It can unite many more people than normal physical space, but you need to adapt the ritual so that participants can sense the energy and feel part of the ritual as if they were there in person. If the ritual isn't adapted for cyberspace, participants will feel like they're sitting in their living rooms reading a ritual onscreen instead of as if they're plugged into cyberspace raising energy and worshipping as a group.

HTTP://MHUINET/~DSPRAGUE/TIAREF.HTML

To Julia, the idea of revising old rituals and designing new ones for cyberspace was intriguing. It also made a lot of sense. Neopagans were a minute portion of the world's population. It was impossible to gather enough of them together to do a proper ritual in some parts of the world, but on the Web, a gathering was only a few keystrokes away. She signed on to TIAMAT-L and gleaned tips on virtual spirituality from its participants.

Many kinds of neopagan spirituality were taking place on the Web. Julia was attracted by what her fellows believed were the magical effects of involvement in a MOO. MOOs are multiuser dimensions of cyberspace. In a MOO, cyber-casters create rooms, objects, and things through textual description that they then move around in. They can also exchange messages with each other in real time. One adept MOOer described the effect of neopagan MOOing as a blending of the virtual and the real:

I learned a few things about how magic can work over Internet connections, although hardly a fraction of what I'd like to learn. A lot more of my knowledge, oddly, came from role-playing online: I learned that you can be drawn into the plots and events you create, and live in that world with a focus it's hard to find in "real life."

HTTP://WWW.BOMBDIGGITY.COM/SHRAPNEL/RITUAL.HTML

Julia also discovered guidelines for setting up activities in cyberspace likely to create this effect. Some neopagan adepts held rituals where everyone gathered in a room with multiple terminals and went online at the same time. According to advanced cyber-neopagans, the goal of these

Give Me That Online Religion

88

gatherings was to create sacred space in cyberspace. But Julia saw it differently. To her, neopagan cyber-rituals acknowledged a sacrality that was already present.

Dream MOOing

The cyberspace mysticism that most impressed Julia was the Dream MOO Project. Julia found the recorded memories of the Dream MOO on what appeared to be a discarded Website. Using a playful "Renaissance Faire" English that marked the comedic turn of the best neopagan practice, the welcome page of the Dream MOO Project recounted the history of the cyber-ritual experiment:

Herein lye thee remains of the DreamMOO Project, thee residua of my mail capture of our various dreams and the associated following ritual. To explore thee dreams for yeself go hence. For thee most recent rounds check DreaMOO 3.1, 3.2, and 3.3. Thee ritual which started it all follows.

PURPOSE: To explore the natural Internet, the collective subconscious

INTENT: To have the participants of the ritual to gather in the collective subconscious, meet and basically MOO.

HTTP://CSBH.MHV.NET/~DSPRAGUE/DM/MAIN.HTML

The Dream MOO Project was an attempt by cyber-neopagans to create a shared, synchronized, lucid dream of the common space and the communal interaction integral to a MOO. In other words, they tried have a cyberspace communal experience without the electricity, without the computer, without the Net.

The site gave specific instructions for how to have a dream MOO. It included requiring everyone to go to bed whenever they needed to so that they could all fall asleep at the same time. The ritual itself was spelled out in detail:

THE RITUAL

The ritual pretty much is falling asleep and entering REM. When you begin to dream or think you are dreaming, do something that will bend that dream's reality. Make your skin green, grow hair where polite people don't grow hair, whatever. Once you have achieved a sense of lucidity in a dream, picture a door in front of you.

Open the door and enter it, in this realm you should introduce yourself to everything that catches your attention or approaches you. This is how I expect everyone to connect in the collective unconscious. Remember, the person you meet maybe won't look like a person to you, they may be a tree or a telephone pole or a pineapple.

When you are in a sizable group of other dreamers, say hello and do whatever you would do in a dream with people who'll play with you in a dream. In the conscious world, about 5–7 hours after you drift off to slumberland, the person who is checking on you should wake you up, but ONLY when you are REMMING. . . . When you are awakened straight out of REM sleep, you remember your dreams better, this will fascilitate [sic] the conscious world to realize if the ritual came off. As soon as you are awakened, write down whatever you dreamed of and who you dreamed you met.

HTTP://CSBH.MHV.NET/~DSPRAGUE/DM/MAIN.HTML

From the site links she could follow, Julia was unable to ascertain whether the cyber-MOO ritual was successful because several links had been deactivated. For a while, she longed to know whether the cyber-MOO dreamers reached each other by way of a non-Internet MOO. Later, she decided that she preferred the unknownness of it. The cyber-MOO was a slippery possibility, like cyberspace-based magic itself. Cyber-MOOing was a mystery to her, but she considered it good to have mysteries in one's life.

As she expanded her involvement as a cyberspace witch, Julia also studied how those outside the neopagan community were working with virtual spirit magic. One of her favorite sites, Lakota, was dedicated to Native American spirituality. Julia ran across it one day when she was flying through cyberspace looking for kindred spirits. She bookmarked Lakota, with plans to return and check it out sometime in the future.

Give Me That Online Religion

When she returned, she decided not only to investigate but to test its spiritual acuity as well. Julia had just been offered a part-time research job, doing field observations of area grade schools for one of the faculty's research projects. Her primary interest was in criminal justice, not the sociology of education. The research project, though interesting, threatened to take her in a direction she did not want to go. But like almost all graduate students Julia knew, she could use the extra money that a research assistantship would bring. Caught in hesitation, Julia logged on to the Lakota site.

It was as interesting as she had remembered. It began with an abbreviated description of why the site designer attributed its contents to the Lakota:

The Lakota, members of the family of the Great Sioux Nation of North America, have a very rich spirituality and a deep respect for all life, visible and invisible. The word Lakota means "considered friends" or "alliance of friends." For these two reasons I felt that the term was most appropriate for this project.

HTTP://WWW.ELEXION.COM/LAKOTA/

Cheryl Harleston, the Lakota Web designer, also provided an explanation of the purpose of the site:

There is a way of living that Native Americans call "to Walk in." It is said that one Walks in Beauty when one has Earth (physicality) and Sky (spirituality) in Harmony. Lakota's intention is to Walk in Beauty. May Wakan Tanka, the Great Mystery, enlighten our path.—Cheryl Harleston

LAKOTA@ELEXION.COM

The Lakota site's heady mix of Native American and neopagan themes resonated well with Julia. Eager to begin, Julia pressed further into the site and came upon a page devoted to rune reading. The page displayed a set of twenty-four virtual runes (letterlike characters) organized in three rows of eight each. The virtual runes looked as if they had been carved from pale wood. There were instructions for how to cyber-cast runes below the virtual rune image:

To get an answer, concentrate on the issue that concerns you at this moment. I suggest that you don't use a question format ("Should I sell the house?"), but rather present the issue ("The issue is the sale of the house"). Once the issue is clear in your mind, click on a Rune. Listen to your intuition!

HTTP://WWW.ELEXION.COM/LAKOTA/READINGS/READING2.HTM

Julia concentrated on what she wanted to know. Her issue was the new job. For five minutes, she meditated on the words "new job," repeating them to herself as a mantra over and over again. Once the echoes had saturated her consciousness, she felt ready to pick her rune. She looked at set of virtual runes displayed on the monitor, lightly moving her mouse pointer in lazy circles over them. After three or four passes, she felt one of the runes in the top row on the left side drawing her pointer toward it, so she clicked on it. When she did, the rune was turned over. The design it displayed was a crowing rooster. The explanation given for the crowing rooster symbol was that it meant an emphatic yes. Julia took the job. A week later, she contacted a coven of cyber-neopagans and made plans to hold her own cyber-MOO. Julia was a cyber-witch.

Online Religion: Some Evaluations

Interreligious tension provoked by misunderstanding has been a contributing cause to outbreaks of violence throughout human history. To the extent extremists succeed in implementing a separatist agenda, the diversity of modern societies thrusts us into a social world of enormous, continuous conflict. However, virtual rituals such as the Cyber-Seder and virtual retreat centers such as Christ in the Desert offer an interesting alternative. By making important aspects of their religion public, traditional religions can employ CMC as both a buffer and an information device. It is unclear whether those who lead traditional religions will adopt virtual rituals as a viable vehicle for human spirituality, but they could have a promising future as a passageway to better interreligious understanding.

To Julia, cyberspace is a medium enabling a new generation of human spirituality to be actualized. These people interact with cyberspace as a site for spiritual exploration and spiritual development. An irresistible idea of a place that captures the religious imagination, cyberspace is a sacred place to which they boldly go, with glee. Though currently a marginal activity in the panorama of online religion, Julia's inventive cyber-quests may prove the most significant online religious activity of all. They hint at the emergence of a new religious role: the cyber-mystic.

Cyber-Virtue and Cyber-Vice

Determining how to apply universal values such as good and evil to virtual territory is a priority for religionists.

Cyberspace expands the range of human behavior beyond the reach of our inherited moral imagination. Less than two decades ago, few knew it was possible to do things such as spam, hack, crack, or flame, much less carry out MOO rape or information terrorism. Today, these and other Internet-spawned antisocial behaviors demonstrate the existence of a dangerous gap in our reigning ideas of good and evil, right and wrong. In exploring the horizon of Internet religion, we must take a close look at how moral concepts such as good and evil, virtue and vice are being applied to online activity. Good and evil, virtue and vice are moral or spiritual concepts rather than legal ones. While lawyers and governments bicker over who can legally do what in cyberspace, determining how to apply universal values such as good and evil to virtual territory is a priority for religionists.

Throughout much of the past, ethical codes have been a contribution of religion to civil society, so it is reasonable to expect that traditional religions would generate the ethical resources necessary to redress online moral lacunae. But as yet, they have not done so. Contributions by traditional religious ethicists to online moral deliberation are rare. Instead, the ethics of cyberspace are emerging out of a moral matrix present in the online world itself. Propelled by their quasi-religious reverence for cyberspace, a small coterie of dedicated computer users offer new moral voices. These pioneers in virtual ethics are struggling to define concepts of good and evil, virtue and vice, adequate to the online world.

How Online Ethics Began

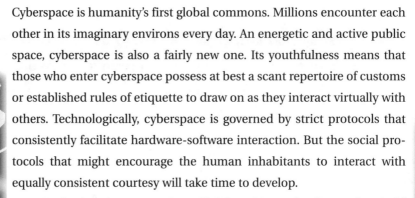

Cyberspace is humanity's first global commons. Millions encounter each other in its imaginary environs every day. An energetic and active public space, cyberspace is also a fairly new one. Its youthfulness means that those who enter cyberspace possess at best a scant repertoire of customs or established rules of etiquette to draw on as they interact virtually with others. Technologically, cyberspace is governed by strict protocols that consistently facilitate hardware-software interaction. But the social protocols that might encourage the human inhabitants to interact with equally consistent courtesy will take time to develop.

In the interim, a set of unofficial working rules have taken hold among heavy online users. They amounted to the first online ethics. Directions for use that minimized the potential for miscommunication, the golden guidelines of cyberspace communication included the following:

⌘ Write in lowercase letters unless you intend your message to be read as a shout.

⌘ Keep posts as short as possible.

⌘ Use *emoticons* to convey emotional context—an example is the three-character string :-) that when viewed sideways resembles a smile and signifies humorous or benign intent.

⌘ Use acronyms such as BTW ("by the way") and IMHO ("in my humble opinion") to help keep messages short.

As helpful as the golden guidelines were, they fell far short of a genuine cyberspace ethic. How short became keenly obvious as the number of Internet-related ethical dilemmas increased. Online child pornography was an obvious vice, but what about "Jenni-Cam," which invited online viewers to check out the activities of a young woman at any time, day or night?[1] Questions arose over whether Internet ethics changed with cyberspace locale. In the free-for-all of a public chat room or in the imaginary world of a MOO, people were expected, if not required, to adopt a persona; but a group of AOL cyber-conversationalists felt completely betrayed when they learned that one of their number who claimed to be a physically handicapped woman was actually a fully abled man.[2]

> [Hacking] begged an important moral question: By going online, does one completely abandon the classic notions of privacy?

The Internet is the ultimate vehicle of public self-expression. But what should our moral response be to those who use it to advocate violence, sexism, racism, or neo-Nazism? To those who attempt to undercut civil authority by virtually publishing classified information? What ethical framework is applicable to measure the moral worth of students being paid to post their class notes on the Web? What are the ethical implications of the fact that almost every online corporation silently inserts "cookies" into the software of those who access their Websites, to track subsequent Web activity?

"Information wants to be free" was a popular motto among the first generation of hackers. They boasted of the ability to access or hack into any online database, regardless of how carefully guarded it was. The hacker myth was that those who accessed closed Websites were the moral cowboys of cyberspace. They cut down the fences that blocked the virtual free range. But this begged an important moral question: By going online, does one completely abandon the classic notions of privacy? The hacker Mixter justified his attacks on computer networks by claiming that they helped reveal a system's vulnerabilities;[3] however, just because someone can break into your house does not mean that the person is on morally solid ground to do so. Is one's Website the same as one's house? In each case, the question of what kind of public arena cyberspace is, and what constitutes right and wrong behavior within it, remain a murky blur.

Religious Ethics

A paramount distinction of religious ethics is that moral judgments are founded in an ultimate principle of the universe. Disagreements among religionists arise over whether that principle is God or Torah or the Bible or the church. But as a religious deliberator, each believes an ultimate principle exists against which human actions can, should, and must be weighed. This does not mean that religious ethicists have an easy time of it. They are challenged by the diverse contexts in which moral dilemmas arise.

By altering the spectrum of human behavior, new technology introduces novel moral situations that confound the customary application of any ultimate principle. At times, the answers to those questions can seem relatively clear, though later analysis may prove that initial clarity misguided. The CAT scan was a new medical technology that expanded our capacity to heal. This seems a straightforward good until questions arose as to whether biases exist in the availability of this costly technology or whether a comparable investment in a less expensive technology might improve the quality of human life more equitably.

Occasionally, the moral valence of a new technology is particularly hard to decipher, especially as the range of activities associated with it develop. Readily embedded in daily life, communicative technologies have been exceptionally fruitful in this regard, pushing the edge of moral thinking. The personal video camera is a banner example. Introduced as a consumer product that enabled families to produce their own home movies quickly and simply, the personal video camera rapidly became a vehicle for original ways of being virtuous, as well as new forms of vice; it spawned a new genre in mass-mediated entertainment on the side.

The innovations in virtue that the personal video camera made possible came to global attention on March 3, 1991, when an amateur photographer near the scene of motorist Rodney King's arrest tape-recorded eighty-one seconds of King's being subdued by police officers. The tape was turned over to area television stations and recurrently broadcast. In the legal trial of the police officers that followed, the defense team undermined the videotape by vivisecting it. They stopped the tape frame by frame and argued that these still shots showed no violation of the law on the part of the officers. But the repeated airing on TV of the in-motion videotape, with its stark violence, hardened public resolve that police treatment of minority motorists be addressed. When the initial trial jury found the officers not guilty—suggesting that this resolve would be thwarted—a series of populist uprisings plunged Los Angeles into chaos for days, and similar incidents broke out in cities across the United States.

By altering the spectrum of human behavior, new technology introduces novel moral situations that confound the customary application of any ultimate principle.

The communication technologies that make possible new forms of virtue also engender new forms of sin. The video camera that facilitated new ways to be a neighbor to someone in distress made it easier to be a pornographer, and it provided the means to invade the privacy of daily life on a heretofore unimaginable scale. Less than two decades after introduction of the video camera, it was impossible to do something as minor as buy a pack of gum without being videotaped.

As the imaginative outgrowth of new media technologies, cyberspace presents those who enter it with a dizzying array of unique moral situations. Confronted with them, online religion is one way people are creating new approaches to the good, as well as a multitude of new ways to sin. Inherently interactive and unavoidably communal, the virtual spiritual communities of cyberspace are enabling people around the world to engage in innovative methods of loving, befriending, and comforting each other, while the same technology is allowing people to betray, ignore, and harm each other and themselves in novel ways as well.

Complicating the moral landscape of cyberspace is its sheer newness as a site of human interaction. The imaginative component of cyberspace makes it readily possible for people to meet there with vastly different perceptions of the moral horizon of their encounter. In some instances, the variance has no bearing. Online child pornography is clearly virtual vice. But in other situations, it can be quite challenging to ascertain exactly what constitutes virtue or sin in an online encounter where how traditional religious beliefs and standards apply is uncertain.

Take as an example the traditional religious code that extramarital sexual involvement is the vice of adultery. Does exchanging online posts containing flirtatious sexual rhetoric with a consenting adult whom one has never met count as having sex? If so, does a married person who exchanges erotic post with someone other than a spouse commit traditional adultery, or some other, new variation—a virtual adultery whose penances have yet to be defined? If not, what exactly is it? How should online textual attempts at seduction, threat, or inducement to illegal behavior be morally understood? Assessed? Valued?

It gets murkier in the intentionally imaginary locales of cyberspace. Does a programmatic or textual assault on a fictional character in a MOO count as assault? Cyberspace requires the evolution of virtual ethics, with its own expectations, boundaries, and sanctions. A site for the boundless expression of human ingenuity, cyberspace raises endless moral questions that online religious communities are working to answer.

The Ethical Outlooks of Cyberspace

If we hike across the moral landscape of cyberspace, we can identify four distinct ethical outlooks emerging from online religious practice. Each poses an understanding of virtual vice and virtue that accords with its worldview.

First are the virtual utopians. Techno-idealists, virtual utopians view the imaginative, electronic realm of cyberspace as a rich site for innovative moral practice. Displaying the zeal of true believers, virtual utopians have no doubt that the World Wide Web constitutes an ideal terrain, a New Jerusalem of electrons only a computer screen away. Though they can be intriguingly nonsectarian, virtual utopians exhibit an evangelistic bent. Not content merely to build utopias in cyberspace, virtual utopians strive to convince the world that cyberspace is the ultimate environment, an Eden blessed with a virtual collage of discourse, sound, and images.

The second outlook is that of virtual anarchists. These people understand cyberspace as a new-style wilderness, a place where community norms and standards do not and should not apply. In keeping with their refusal to submit to organized rule, a great diversity exists among virtual anarchists. Some are benevolent and creative social misfits, fashioning themselves as protectors of cyberspace as the last free frontier. Others are malevolently inclined and want cyberspace to function as a law-free zone where corrupt activity can go on undetected and unpunished.

The third major outlook is held by virtual tourists. These people foray into cyberspace like amateur mountaineers climbing Mount Everest as a quest for adventure. Virtual tourists seek a peak experience from what they encounter there, but they also get into serious trouble. Inexperienced yet craving novelty, virtual tourists become engaged in online exchanges that pull them into a moral quagmire they are ill-prepared to address.

Fourth are the virtually oblivious. These are people who regularly appear online but who do not treat cyberspace as a viable site of moral (or any other kind of) practice.

Right now, all four moral outlooks on the virtual universe are manifestly evident in cyberspace. Those who espouse and enact their interpretation of the value and meaning of online activity are, rather unsystematically, shaping our habits of practice in relationship to cyberspace and in turn influencing the formulation of new laws to regulate it.

Along with sketching these outlooks in more detail, this chapter introduces some of the denizens of each one and explores the distinct varieties of sin and goodness each is working to construct virtually. As we visit these diverse, apparently incompatible moral terrains, it becomes evident that cyberspace is not a unified moral community. Instead, it harbors a number of incommensurate ethical systems; some bear relevance to nonvirtual life, but others apply exclusively to the virtual environment.

Virtual Utopians

Like seventeenth-century Puritans fleeing England for America, some people enter cyberspace for the express purpose of founding a utopian community there. One of the better-known assemblages of virtual utopians is the Well (www.well.com). Established in 1988, the Well was set up by people associated with the *Whole Earth Review* as a hosted, online experimental community. It was the express goal of its founders that the Well be a site fostering social change.[4] Many early hosts of the Well were people experienced in organizing and managing real-life experimental utopian groups.

As notably documented by Howard Rheingold, the Well was a prototype virtual utopia whose community participants, with the encouragement of the online host, shared information that helped nurse one another to health, made each other more efficient at work, and mourned one another in death.[5]

Not all virtual utopias are founded quite so intentionally. Some develop offhandedly, as accidental utopias. Femrel-l is one such group.[6]

Many of those involved with femrel-l first got involved while doing graduate study. Hannah was one. Doing graduate work in critical theory at a northern California university, she worked as a university research fellow twenty hours a week while taking a full-time load of graduate courses. She found herself spending a sizable portion of each day entering data into a computer. Overall, according to work logs, Hannah interacted with a computer an average of thirty hours a week over the course of several years, compiling field notes, documenting research interviews, maintaining class notes, and writing graduate papers.

This effort paid off well for her in terms of furthering her career goals. She finished graduate school, got her first teaching job, and wrote and defended a dissertation in slightly over five years, simultaneously completing a huge quantity of field research. But the work dedication that moves careers forward can throw personal lives into a tailspin. The tasks she was assigned as a researcher required that she become adept at distancing herself from social dynamics to critically observe them. It also required her to spend an extraordinary amount of time apart from others documenting these findings. As she moved toward the professional goals she sought, her key personal relationships dissolved.

Spending more time with a computer than with any human being (not to mention "any animal, vegetable, mineral, or other technological product," as Hannah acerbically observed), she became curious about whether it was possible to make social connections *using* her computer, not in spite of it. Hannah regularly surfed the Web for information as well as just to see what was there. Like countless others spending more hours per week with computers than human beings, she began seeking sociability in cyberspace with little idea of who or what she might find there.

What she found was femrel-l, a paramount assembly of virtual utopians. At the simplest level, femrel-l is merely an unmoderated, online discussion list. Anyone who wants to can subscribe. A would-be participant merely needs to send an e-mail message to the femrel-l listserv and ask to join. All who become femrel-l subscribers, however, are invited to participate in an imaginary world of incredible word-play delight. Before a day passes, femrel-l subscribers can find themselves designing femrel-l T-shirts, planning a gathering, or jumping into a virtual hot tub for a relaxing, round-the-world soak with contributors from Australia. (In the second month of Hannah's femrel-l involvement, Rosalind and Jay, two people who subscribed to the list but lived thousands of miles apart, decided that they were meant for each other. To the supportive virtual cheering of the list, Jay visited and then moved to the same town as Rosalind. A real-life romance was born.)

To Hannah, participating in femrel-l's virtual utopia was easy. She merely read posts to the lists; nearly everyone involved was what leading sociologists of religion describe as a "free rider."[7] That is, the bulk of subscribers took the goods of femrel-l (essentially, its provocative, rolling, at times riotously funny conversation) without contributing much, if anything, in return. Although the total subscriber population averaged well over one hundred and occasionally exceeded three hundred, a core of twenty femrel-l-ers generated the bulk of the traffic in conversation on the list.

After finding femrel-l, Hannah began looking forward to the time she spent on her computer. As a break from her job-related writing, she would log on to the Internet and read the magical, mysterious, provocative discourse of the unknown and unseen participants. Occasionally she wondered why the conversations were much more stimulating than typical face-to-face dialogue. Gradually she concluded that it was because femrel-l only required its members to be utopian intermittently—as soon as you logged on and only while you were online. Afterward, participants went back to their quotidian life, where there were dishes to be washed, a dog that needed flea dipping, and a partner who did not necessarily respond with the élan of a virtual correspondent.

When Hannah's graduate study was completed, her work as a new college professor kept her extremely busy. As she became accustomed to the high interaction of classroom teaching, she withdrew from her online utopian involvement.

Certain intrinsic aspects of cyberspace help femrel-l and its ilk build such viable, albeit virtual, utopias. Cyberspace is available twenty-four hours a day, seven days a week; computer lists never close. Since cyberspace is global rather than geographically limited, its citizenry can be quite diverse. Femrel-l membership was eclectic, including Muslims, Jews, neopagans, evangelical Christians, Mormons, and none of the above. During one extended period, it even included the chaplain at Duke University. This diversity was possible only because of cyberspace's unique electronic, delocalized, interactive publicity. If femrel-l had a geography-based identity, such eclectic diversity would have been unlikely, if not impossible.

Innovative virtual utopians are generating countless new forms of virtue, of doing good for and to others. On femrel-l, new virtues include posting messages to "send energy" to those in distress and an immense amount of spiritual play to relieve tedium and frustration. Another flourishing spiritual practice in cyberspace virtual utopias is online prayer. This includes online prayer chains and chat rooms and e-prayer wheels. (An e-prayer is read by holding down the scroll button as a prayer-blessing dances over the screen.)

The first tenet of any virtual utopia's ethical code is that participants be honest in what they write, that is, honestly describe themselves and their life situation. The second is that contributors write clearly and cleverly, in an aphoristic style, and mostly in lowercase letters. Long posts are acceptable, but short, concise posts are infinitely preferable. The third is that each participant be open to the contributions of all others and respond in a manner that encourages total community involvement. This does not mean that someone who signs on to the list for the first time (known as a "newbie") is expected to describe every personal aspect in excruciating detail; however, it does mean that list members expect the accounts participants give of themselves to be true.

In virtual utopias, sin consists of violating these tenets. This is why, when participants in an online utopian discussion are discovered to have been deceptive or misleading in their self-presentation, a backlash against the masked participant occurs. Regular practice of utopian virtues makes these ideal cyber-communities possible. Their absence or violation erodes the utopian experience and threatens the community with dissolution.

The first tenet of any virtual utopia's ethical code is that participants be honest in what they write, that is, honestly describe themselves and their life situation.

The situation is the diametrical opposite in expressly imaginative online virtual environments such as MOOs. Dedicated to role playing, multiuser play societies are, conversely, places where participants are expected to disguise their identity; they would be deemed quite odd if they did not. Thus the definition of sin and virtue in a virtual utopia is directly related to the purpose and goals of its founding. If a virtual utopia is formed to create an electronic haven, virtual hospitality flourishes. The people involved fashion e-toasts, send each other e-treats, and devise elaborate e-welcome messages, and sin is whatever detracts from or interferes with these practices.

Because morality in virtual utopias is frequently determined by situational ethics, virtual utopias give a rather postmodernist cast to cyberspace. To the extent that this is not the case, it is a possibility primarily restrained by the permeability of cyberspace itself. Virtual utopias may form tight virtual social bonds, but since virtual utopias meet in cyberspace, their gatherings cannot be isolated and are not physically accessible. It is therefore difficult for them to silence outsiders or to shut out divergent voices. To persist as virtual utopian communities, participants must accept that there are always strangers in their midst. Even though this may impinge on their ability to achieve the quality of utopian experience the true believers might want, it also makes them less rigid utopias than many of the real-life experiments in human communal living—and it may contribute to their endurance.

Virtual Anarchists

The vast majority of virtual anarchists are libertarians who consider cyberspace the New American West. Philosophically, they conceive of cyberspace as a wilderness, an untamed and untamable virtual frontier where no laws can or should apply.

Benevolently inclined virtual anarchists are seriously committed to the absolute freedom they believe should typify life in cyberspace. Dedicated to preserving absolute online freedom as an inalienable human right, they can be considered a wild strain of the virtual utopian. Malevolent virtual anarchists desire an absence of law or any type of regulation in cyberspace so they can more readily harm and abuse others. In between are those virtual anarchists who fight any restriction of cyberspace so that they can use the easy publicity of cyberspace to do things they would not do IRL.

Jason was one of the most benevolent virtual anarchists in cyberspace. He was as well the variety of virtual anarchist with which the general public is most familiar: a hacker. After completing two years of college coursework in computer science at a large midwestern state university, he fled to the growing city of Phoenix, where he knew his dexterous touch with any computer he approached would make him eminently employable. His confidence was justified. In an industry propelled by rapid change, someone with Jason's abilities and people skills could always land work somewhere. Phoenix proved no exception. Within a week after arriving, he landed a job that paid more than many of his tenured college professors were making back home.

By day, Jason labored away at his new post, troubleshooting the computers of top executives of a major software manufacturer. By night, he was a dedicated hacker. Using the hacker's motto—"information wants to be free"—as his moral sextant, he sailed across the virtual oceans of cyberspace nearly every night, trying to locate critical sites that refused entry to outsiders; he would then do whatever it took to get in.

Virtual anarchists conceive of cyberspace as a wilderness, where no laws can or should apply.

Jason was truly committed to being a benevolent hacker. He took incredible pains to never hurt the systems he entered. Where some of his fellow hackers got their thrills demonstrating their computer prowess by hacking into people's personal files (such as the medical records of the rich and famous), Jason steered clear of such invasion of privacy. Instead, he hunted for the hacker's big game: hidden government files, not-yet-released videos, and—best of all—new computer games not yet brought to market.

To Jason, hacking was a virtue, not a sin. "To me, cyberspace is free space," he says. "It was built with American taxpayers' dollars. So whatever is in it is free, at least free to play with. Getting through corporate security systems is a game, like virtual chess. Most of the fun I have is in figuring out what the system I am up against will do . . . and telling my friends about it afterward."

The other well-known type of virtual anarchist is the flamer. This is the person who sends explosively hostile e-mail posts. Their meaning is so volatile it is as if the words are on fire. There may be a sliver of virtual anarchy in the mind of each inhabitant of cyberspace, for in addition to the fairly common experience of receiving a flame, almost no one who participates in the online world manages to escape the embarrassment of eventually posting one.

In cyberspace, sites dedicated to online pornography and erotica wrap themselves like kudzu about and around the virtual environment. Given their pervasive presence, we are as likely to run into a sex-related sin site accidentally as on purpose, which poses a considerable hazard for the virtual tourist.

The content of sex sin sites ranges from the banal to the outrageous and the profoundly disturbing. Among the banal are the endless nude photos of actresses and actors—Sherry and Pamela, John and Trevor. Some of these actually depict the individuals they claim to represent; others are virtual constructs. The fight to keep such images out of this harvest for the virtual voyeur has spawned a new field of employment: hiring people to track down sites that purport to offer nude photos of celebrities and threatening to sue if the offenders do not pull the photo offline.

Also in the column of the outrageous are online video camera sex sites. A camera is trained on a seller of virtual sex set up in a remote site, and virtual Johns log on. For a fee, they can request their virtual prostitute to engage in a variety of activities.

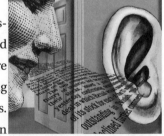

In the register of the profoundly disturbing are sex sin sites that promote child pornography, as well as those set up to lure children into sex talk—and even to agreeing to sexual assignations with online predators.

Arch humor characterizes some sin sites. Underneath headlines that boldly declare the site to be dedicated to sin is copy with claims so outrageously overblown that they beg the readers to laugh and not take themselves or the site seriously. Adopting P. T. Barnum's reigning philosophy ("There's a sucker born every minute"), comedic sin sites tend to employ popular Christian elements associated with sin such as the devil, hell, and the soul, playfully using language that "true believers" treat with reverence and awe. In the press, they invite people to engage in a game of spiritual "chicken."

The Sell Your Soul site strikingly demonstrates the comedic, teenage, "dare you" approach that certain Web spinners employ when dealing with ancient taboos in the realm of human spirituality. The site mocks the reader with dark black and red graphics that spout words like *blood* and *evil*. Then it slyly invites visitors to prove they are jaded modernists by doing something no one who declares evil to be real would do: they invite you to sell your soul.

SELL YOUR SOUL.

EvilPeople, INC.™ is always willing to add to the Unholy Might™ of the nether regions, and one of the ways that we can do this is to, well, buy your soul. Since most of you puny mortals have rather materialistic desires, EvilPeople, INC.™ is more than willing to provide you with them. And we just want one teensy-weensy little thing in return.

HTTP://WWW.GAIJIN.COM/EVILPEOPLE/CONTRACT.HTML

Visitors are then invited to click a button and sell their souls. It is a spoof, of course, but a psychologically clever one. Toying with the language of eternal fate, the Website dares you to call its bluff.

Another famous comedic sin site is the Dark Lair of Infinite Evil. In a subsite, it boasts "attractions" such as the Great Wall of Evil, where you publicly post a curse on anyone you wish. The site also contains a rant section where the author of the site, Joseph L. Mitchell III, complains about people who have written to him and tried to convert him:

During the time that the Dark Lair of Infinite Evil has been in existence, several of my more self-righteous visitors have made assumptions about my personal beliefs based upon the content of these pages which I have authored. Regardless of my ACTUAL beliefs, these people have found it necessary to act on their assumptions and to try to convert me to their way of thinking (which is OBVIOUSLY the only "correct" beliefs to have, right?). This page is a tribute to those poor misguided individuals who are closed-minded enough to not see past the end of their own brown noses.—J. L Mitchell

HTTP://WWW.DMA.ORG/CGI-BIN/CGIWRAP/
MITCHELJ/DESECRATE/EVIL/

A committed virtual anarchist with a comedic bent, Mitchell relishes his role as a cyberspace provocateur on the topic of evil. He strives to vanquish any critics with quips and puns. His Evil Website clearly demonstrates the energy that virtual anarchists tap, which is considered to be the cardinal virtue of their existence. To virtual anarchists, sin is any acknowledgment of what Freud described as the discontents of civilization. Repression is for land people. In the virtual world, only the limits of your imagination, your hardware, and your software need rule.

Virtual anarchists include some of the most troubling members of the virtual world. The anarchists are also some of its most creative contributors. Their intense celebration of freedom as virtue has moved those under its aegis to produce search engines, browsers, and a host of freeware that has been given, gratis, to the world. Yet because virtual anarchists equate sin with restraint, they produce sites quite inappropriate for younger virtual tourists and indulge in online activities such as cracking (breaking into restricted sites and altering data) that are unquestionably wrong. When it comes to virtual anarchy, it is difficult to imagine the online world without these people yet almost impossible to live in the global community with them.

Virtual Tourists

Poignant moral problems also arise from involvement in the online environment by virtual tourists. These people are viscerally attracted to cyberspace, finding it an instance of irresistible mystery. They quickly become virtual tourists, investing copious quantities of time exploring the vast unknown virtual universe. Like tourists who travel to geographical sites with which they are unfamiliar, they can—and do—get into trouble, sometimes a great deal of trouble, before they quite realize it.

Venturing into unfamiliar relationships, interactions, and activities, virtual tourists act and behave like people who do not know the lay of the land. They get lost. They say the wrong things. Young children constitute much of the virtual tourist population, which is why they may need maps or browser filters to keep them out of harm's way.

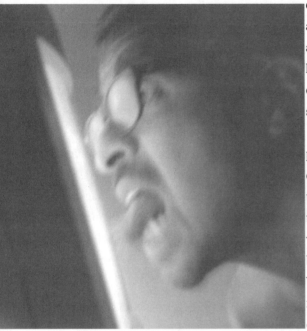

One of the first places virtual tourists go is to an online chat room. Logging in can be something like walking into a Halloween costume party that has been under way for several hours. It is not clear who anyone is. Ribald exchanges go on everywhere. The actual character of those present is completely ambiguous. To a virtual tourist, it is not clear how to join a conversation—or even whether one should do so, given how raucous they can sometimes be.

In an online chat room, anything can happen while "nothing" happens. The anything that can happen includes textual seduction, as illustrated in the popular movie *You've Got Mail*. In the film, Kelly, played by Meg Ryan, whimsically visits an "over thirty" chat room on her thirtieth birthday, where she meets Joe (Tom Hanks). Writing online messages to each other that give no personal details and are inscribed with pseudonyms, the two discover that they have a lot in common and commence writing to each other daily. Soon the posts Kelly and Joe exchange constitute the most important human contact either person experiences, even though each is romantically involved with another. Reflecting unacknowledged guilt in the pleasure they derive from their online exchanges, both Kelly and Joe make sure their lovers are long gone before they sit down at their computers to compose and read messages to and from each other.

In *You've Got Mail*, the deepening online intimacy between Kelly and Joe is presented as posing no substantial moral dilemmas. Their real-life romantic partners are shown to be inadequate mates whom they would be better off leaving. In fact, to clear an absolutely pristine path for Kelly and Joe, the screenwriters allow the pair's discarded love attachments to become attracted to one another before Kelly and Joe get seriously involved. This makes it appear not merely acceptable for the central characters to pursue their romantic online relationship but actually justifiable.

Like real-life tourists, virtual tourists are occasionally motivated to embark on a journey because of painful events at home. Melanie was an example, reeling from the unexpected loss of her partner and turning to cyberspace for solace. What she encountered there was so positive, it made the problems "back home" bearable:[8]

A year ago (a year ago exactly tomorrow, in fact) my partner of almost 5 years left me and I was in a lot of pain. The breakup came pretty abruptly, and sent me reeling into a second year of hell. The first year of hell was probably a major cause of the second. It was the year after my partner's nephew came up to live with us. He'd been badly abused, and was angry and violent. He was only 9 years old when he came up, but I'd never lived with abuse or its results before, and I had a really hard time dealing with his violence. I was pretty badly depressed during that entire year, and was still having problems with depression (though he was no longer violent) when my partner (a woman, BTW) met another woman, fell "madly in love," and went off with her. I felt pretty desperately betrayed.

Melanie turned to cyberspace for company, and what she found there amazed her:

[I got involved with a private list that] was very instrumental in me dealing with the aftermath of my breakup, and in helping me find a way to strengthen my spiritual/religious life, which I knew from the get-go was crucial. I wrote a lot on that list about my pain, about the history of the relationship, about the history of the breakup. . . . Folks on that list . . . helped me find something that will be with me forever, to my everlasting gratitude.

In sum, virtual tourists can run across troubling and dangerous sex sites, find one another and true love, or stumble into a virtual utopian community and be helped. Like their material counterparts, virtual tourists are in strange territory and don't quite know where the dragons lie.

The Virtually Oblivious

To countless casual computer users as well as to many who have never gone online, discussing cyberspace ethics may seem no more substantial than discussing the Loch Ness monster. Each involves something no one has ever seen, although people insistently speak as if both are real. Amy, a twenty-year-old Italian American majoring in French at a small, private liberal arts college, is an excellent example. She considers herself computer literate. Her ability on a computer superseded that of her parents, who used PCs unimaginatively in their jobs. But halfway through a course on contemporary religious thought, Amy began to wonder if she had ever paid real attention to the computers that had been part of her life since birth. Reading Jennifer Cobb's theology of cyberspace,[9] in which Cobb contends that cyberspace is humanity's attempt to hardwire its physical and mental interdependence, Amy realized she did not think of her computer as something connecting her to cyberspace. One day in class, after reading a long passage about the importance of cyberspace, she exclaimed in frustration, "But I just don't get it. I log on to a computer in the lab, check my e-mail, and then log out. What is this cyberspace thing all about?"

Amy is not alone. Though a rapidly increasing percentage of the population is involved with CMC, the concept of cyberspace remains elusive to a significant portion of them. Their computers are technological tools akin to a car or a TV. They can scarcely grasp that cyberspace is altering their moral values. Like people who stare at optical illusions but fail to see the pattern within, they stare at their computer screens and wonder, "What is this cyberspace thing all about, anyway?"

These users have not developed virtues appropriate to the virtual realm, since they have never recognized cyberspace as a site, much less a site of moral practice. But they *have* developed their own variety of virtual sin. Paying almost no attention to cyberspace as a site of public communicative exchange, the virtually oblivious ignore societal debates over the future of cyberspace, thereby leaving it prone to manipulation and exploitation by those who have grasped and wish to harness its potential—most often for private gain.

The Texture of Virtual Grace and Virtual Sin

Historically, it has been the province of religion to establish the norms that dictate how people should behave in response to moral dilemmas. In certain times and places—medieval Europe, for example—religious institutions fulfilled this role with the aid of philosophy. At other times—as in Classical Greece—religionists and philosophers were at odds over whose voice should be decisive in defining human moral life. However, religion has consistently been the popular favorite and remains the moral source of choice for people the world over. People turn to religion for insight and instruction when confronted with moral dilemma. From Judaism and Christianity to Buddhism and Islam, religious traditions provide their adherents with ethical codes and standards of moral conduct to follow in this world.

The challenge of adapting and applying an inherited set of ancient precepts to one's own unique historical setting is daunting, especially for modern people who must contend with accelerating change.

Some of these religious codes take the form of a system of laws to be observed within a community; the Sharia of Islam is an ancient code of this sort. Others are woven into the central myths of the tradition; in Hinduism, the *Bhagavad Gita* and the *Ramayana* are stories of the gods that function as narrative vehicles to convey the ethical codes of the tradition. To the extent the adherents of a religion follow its ethical code, they gain the assurance that they are behaving rightly in the world—an assurance typically acknowledged in liturgy and rituals. Frequently, they garner additional assurance that they are enhancing their access to the next world, to any life-beyond-life that exists.

The basic tenets of the ethical code of a world religion are so embedded in cultural habits and assumptions that they often function as moral norms or standards, for both adherents of the religion and countless others not directly associated with the sponsoring faith. The Ten Commandments of Judaism and the Golden Rule of Christianity ("Do unto others as you would have others do unto you") are each the centerpiece of an ethical code born in a religious community that later became accepted as a moral imperative by substantial numbers outside the sponsoring religion's adherent population.

Everyone who tries to live in accord with her or his tradition's code must do so in the particular, within the context of the time in which she or he lives. The challenge of adapting and applying an inherited set of ancient precepts to one's own unique historical setting is daunting, especially for modern people who must contend with accelerating change. "Love your neighbor" is a moral axiom that billions espouse, but the question "Who is my neighbor?" was troubling even to those who lived in the days of Jesus (at least according to the gospel stories).

Who Is Our Virtual Neighbor?

In cyberspace, millions of people are only a mouse click away. Are they all our neighbors? Short of a Christian saint or a Buddhist bodhisattva, it is difficult to imagine that normal human compassion can stretch so far. Cyberspace threatens to fulfill Andy Warhol's prophecy that every person on the planet will be famous for fifteen minutes. If even 10 percent dedicate their time on the public stage to airing grievances, what moral obligation do we take on through our encounter with them? Caught up in the cornucopia of contemporary electronic interactivity, one is almost impelled to ask, "Who is my neighbor?" and be somewhat worried about the answer.

> **Caught up in the cornucopia of contemporary electronic interactivity, one is almost impelled to ask, "Who is my neighbor?" and be somewhat worried about the answer.**

If we determine that a cyberspace-facilitated request for help can be safely ignored because of its sender's questionable status as neighbor, we may miss the opportunity that cyberspace offers us to give birth to a moral imagination that encompasses the globe. Each denial of another's need necessarily advances the triumph of injustice over justice. No population facing demands for justice from any marginalized individual or group ever thought the request was timely. Whereas TV opened the door to seeing carefully staged presentations of other cultures, cyberspace puts us in direct, one-on-one contact with neighbors around the world. The challenge we face is how to live up to the moral and ethical dilemmas, both personal and communal, these encounters raise.

Our inherited religious ideas about virtue and vice can help us sort out the ethical dimensions of the online world, but they need to be helped along. After all, to evaluate whether a textual seduction "counts" as adultery, one needs to have some sense of what it actually involves. Does the fact that one's partner writes word symbols on a screen loaded with sexual meaning constitute virtual adultery, or is it the time taken away from a primary relationship that violates the relational bond? If time is the issue, can anyone who heavily invests in an online experience (from a trout fishing Usenet group to an opera chat room) risk being accused of betraying a partner? If so, what does this imply for real-life hobbies as well? Does a promise of sexual fidelity given by partners in a relationship encompass fidelity of the imagination as well as of the body? If so, we may have defined fidelity beyond the ability of any human being to maintain it. Is virtual sexuality harmless flirtation or unacceptable violation?

What about virtual flaming? Should people who compose and unleash textual assaults on others be considered morally reprehensible in some novel way? Is flaming to be considered a different moral order than

> ## The free and easy neighborliness that characterizes a great deal of cyberspace conversation is an incredible testament to the human capacity to love one another—even strangers.

writing a vindictive personal note? Is it more or less morally culpable than penning a potentially damaging newspaper or magazine article? A new body of law is rapidly being assembled to address these quandaries through defining what one *can* do without penalty, but the question of what one *should* do in such situations—the question of ethics and morality, of religious meaning—remains largely unanswered.

As troubling as instances of cyber-vice can be, the marvels of cyber-virtues are comparably impressive. Twenty-four hours a day, people in cyberspace willingly help others, listen to one another's complaints, give each other directions and advice. The free and easy neighborliness that characterizes a great deal of cyberspace conversation is an incredible testament to the human capacity to love one another—even strangers you have never seen and may never meet in your entire life.

Traditional religious codes proffer various precepts to span the meaning gap that arises in a real-life moral quandary; but none possess the goods of meaning that easily address the ethical dilemmas raised in cyberspace by the possibility of virtual sex, virtual friendship, or promo-

Give Me That Online Religion

tion of virtual sin. This spiritual reflection needs to be undertaken by those who know cyberspace and maintain a serious online religious presence (recall Bishop Gaillot, from Chapter Two, or the religious virtuosos associated with well-established virtual utopias). They are resources of new spiritual wisdom to help people sort out virtue and vice in the online world.

One overarching ethical issue of cyberspace involves us all. It is the question of context. It is a public matter to decide whether we want cyberspace to be a "public space" like parks and schools, dedicated to public use with mandated public access, or privatized, commodified, sold off like land targeted for development of a strip mall. These are not necessarily mutually exclusive choices. Through virtual zoning, portions of cyberspace could be dedicated to each contrasting purpose. But this can only happen if people recognize the potential benefits and dangers of cyberspace and become politically active in steering the development of its terrain.

6

CHAPTER

Virtual Shrines and the Cult of Celebrity

It now seems prophetic that the first nonmilitary use of electronically linked computers was for an impassioned discussion by Star Trek fans.

The new millennium is the age of celebrity. It is also the age of the Internet. That is only fitting, as the two phenomena are connected symbiotically. Indeed, among its manifold functions, the Internet serves as a global forum where people can air their interest in and responses to celebrities. It now seems prophetic that the first nonmilitary use of electronically linked computers was for an impassioned discussion of science fiction by *Star Trek* fans.[1] Today in cyberspace, an entire genre of Websites exists whose central purpose is to honor celebrities, fictional characters, or vehicles of entertainment.

Although characterized by highly sophisticated graphics, few of these celebrity sites are professionally produced. The originator is most often an intensely committed fan with a keen capacity for Web design. As soon as a new celebrity site is launched, cyber-travelers who share the originator's passion quickly find it. If the site is sufficiently appealing, fellow fans congregate in its chat room and link the site to their homepage. Some build complementary pages that expand the group's knowledge base. Within a short period, a virtual fan subculture has emerged.

Expressed in a Babel of languages, these sites bear testimony to the striking phenomenon of celebrity devotion. The content of these celebrity Websites suggests that for many people, celebrities are much more than admired. They are adored. They are emulated. They are studied and followed. There are Websites that welcome you to the Church of Elvis and others that proclaim the millennial future of *Star Trek*. One celebrity site encourages people to live life according to the example of *The Brady Bunch*. Another attributes the authority of religious texts to passages from *The X-Files*. When celebrity Websites reach this extreme, their creators have moved beyond fandom into worship. Out of their zeal, they produce virtual temples to the stars.

For anyone enmeshed in celebrity worship, cyberspace is the consummate public space. It is a venue through which people can preach their celebrity passions to the world. Scanning fan sites, it is easy to believe that the spiritual discipline of *imitato Christus* has been replaced by the spiritual discipline of, say, *imitato* Keanu Reeves. Wry puns permeate the liturgy of virtual celebrity. They deflect the simplistic conclusion that celebrity sites manifest serious spiritual intent. But perhaps they should not; Websites designed to adore celebrities may represent virtual play with spirituality through religious language and themes. Alternatively, they may reflect a new religious movement—or a nebulous combination of serious and nonserious intent.

Surely some fan altars are spoofs. Still, the hundreds of thousands of unremunerated hours invested in building and maintaining celebrity altar sites suggest that something more than sheer frivolity is involved. Further, even when a Web designer launches a "tongue-in-cheek" celebrity worship site, there is no guarantee that those who access it will respond as the designer intended. One person's joke can become another's sacred story—as the history of religions repeatedly attests.

> One person's joke can become another's sacred story—as the history of religions repeatedly attests.

One might expect that media megaliths that survive by marketing celebrities would welcome celebrity-inspired popular religions. But that's absolutely not true. Although media corporations feed off the passion of fans, they resist fan initiatives to contribute to "constructing" the celebrities they consume. Copyright arguments between fans and entertainment conglomerates reprise the historical notions of orthodoxy and heresy, only now on an economic playing field. Today no less than in the medieval era, the question of who is authorized to tell stories about particular people is a matter of public concern, debate, and sanction.

Viacom, for instance, aggressively challenges and has legally shut down pieces of fan Websites such as the script excerpts included in the Life According to the Brady Bunch site (www.teleport.com/~btucker/bbsorry.com), claiming they infringe on copyrights or trademarks.[2] Wishing to harness fans' Internet presence for their own purposes, media companies now publish "official" Websites for the actors, characters, and shows they have under contract. In response, fan Websites dutifully note the onset of so-called official sites and go on to criticize them for their emotional flatness and obvious commercial nature.

The Varieties of Virtual Celebrity Worship

Turning to cyberspace to examine the functional religions that celebrity worship inspires, we quickly see that celebrity sites are as different as the celebrities themselves. Still, three types of celebrity site predominate. A *memorial* site seeks to preserve the memory of a celebrity by functioning as a virtual destination for pilgrimage. An *altar* site literally idolizes a celebrity by presenting a framework for cultic devotion. Finally, *community* sites organize fans into congregations. Each reflects the extent to which fandom is a serious source of meaning for billions at the start of the new millennium, a feeder stream into the complex fount of contemporary moral and religious life.

The Memorial Site: Mourning Lady Diana

On the pages of *People* magazine and profiled in the television show *Entertainment Tonight* and the E! cable channel, people are treated as celebrities without distinction. Christian evangelist Billy Graham appears alongside pop star Madonna, world-class cellist Yo-Yo Ma, film actor  Annette Bening, and Darva Conquer (the *Who Wants to Marry a Millionaire?* bride), all with neither editorial nor reader comment. The casualness of such eclectic groupings stems from an unstated assumption: since all of them are celebrities, each is entitled to be treated as a celebrity alongside all the others, even though their individual fame and popularity has been achieved for differing reasons.

Media and public response to Lady Diana and Mother Teresa's nearly coincident deaths in 1997 illustrate how leveling contemporary celebrity can be. Coverage flitting between scenes of Lady Diana's funeral and the pronouncement of Mother Teresa's death on the same day served up an apocalyptic or revelatory moment. It laid bare the extent to which religious figures are celebrities who must compete with other celebrities for airtime, public attention, and even spiritual and moral significance.

In the short run, sometimes they lose. Mother Teresa is likely to attain sainthood in the Roman Catholic Church. If so, memory of her life and work will be carried forward for centuries. Without a comparable institutional base, Lady Diana's fame could fade considerably earlier. At the time of their deaths, however, the celebrity hagiographies produced by the entertainment press made Lady Diana and Mother Teresa equivalent saints. Diana's campaign of public appearances on behalf of land-

Give Me That Online Religion

mine victims was treated with the same virtuous respect as Mother Teresa's decades of labor for the destitute in India. On the day of Lady Diana's funeral and Mother Teresa's death, the front pages of countless newspapers carried equal-sized photos of both.

In cyberspace, however, Lady Diana was the more deeply and widely mourned. Hers are among the most popular memorial sites on the Internet, and it is hard to deny that in the virtual universe, Lady Diana eclipsed Mother Teresa as the perfect embodiment of female piety. Little from their respective biographies hinted of such a legacy. During her brief life, Diana of England garnered a strange, hybrid celebrity. Catapulted to fame as a real-life Cinderella who married a prince, Diana's modern reprise of an ancient fairy tale collapsed en route to what, according to legend, should have been a happily-ever-after ending. Newspapers, magazines, television and radio shows, and Web pages kept the public regularly informed of each bitter fracture in Diana's married life. She suffered from bulimia. She was humiliated by marital betrayal. She committed adultery. Few were surprised when Diana's marriage collapsed and she and her prince divorced.

> It is hard to deny that in the virtual universe, Lady Diana eclipsed Mother Teresa as the perfect embodiment of female piety.

Far from distancing people from her, Diana's suffering, disappointments, and mistakes stimulated millions to relate to her through an identification almost mystical in its intensity. The media obligingly fed public interest. For the last few years of her life, the postdivorce Diana was the most famous woman in the world. An international celebrity, she was ceaselessly sought after by media in every nation she visited. To the shock of the world, she died in a fatal car accident in Paris on August 31, 1997, while her fame was still at its peak. She was thirty-six years old.

Mother Teresa became a figure of global renown during the same period as Lady Diana. She garnered her fame as a distinctly religious personage. She was respected, adored, revered, and sometimes feared in consequence of this fact. Founder of the Missionaries of Charity, a religious order in Calcutta, India, Mother Teresa dedicated her life to caring for the fatally ill poor, helping them die with dignity. Her tireless work on behalf of the most shunned of society inspired moral admiration and awe. Among her many honors, Mother Teresa was awarded the Nobel Peace Prize in 1979.

Like Lady Diana, Mother Teresa was able to connect with the public powerfully. Young university women spent summers in Calcutta serving under her direction. To legions of the poor in India, she was a living saint. People speaking about the outer reaches of human compassion would refer to Mother Teresa as an unsurpassable demonstration of its embodiment. As was the case with Lady Diana, the media responded to public interest. Stories of Mother Teresa's life and ministry became a staple of global news.

Like the ancient tombs of saints and mystics, these virtual effigies pluck strings of remembrance.

On September 5, 1997, as Lady Diana was being laid to rest, Mother Teresa died. The overlap between the two deaths set off a chaotic scramble among journalists assigned to respond to them. Mother Teresa's death evoked genuine mourning among the members of her order and from innumerable others around the world; but Diana's elicited a much broader public response. When the news spread that Diana was dead, people of varying nationalities, ethnic backgrounds, ages, and economic classes stood on street corners and wept. In England, anguish over Diana's demise rose to such heights that the English monarchy altered burial customs and accorded her additional public honors rather than risk condemnation for being indifferent to public sentiment.

The outpouring of mourning devotion in cyberspace for Lady Diana was stunning and immense. By my count, more than eight hundred thousand Websites—an astonishing number in any terms—are dedicated to her memory. Like the ancient tombs of saints and mystics, these virtual

Give Me That Online Religion

effigies pluck strings of remembrance. One impressive memorial site, attributed to Richard E. Begert, is titled "Princess Diana, A Tribute." It opens with a full black screen, etched with a rendering of the Diana rose and a quote from William Shakespeare: "Farewell! Thou art too dear for my possessing. . . ." Scrolling down, one encounters two photos of Diana, one an official princess portrait, set off by the comments of someone identified only as "a viewer":

I just wanted to be among the millions of people who are no doubt congratulating you on your beautiful tribute. I was . . . so very moved by the quality and choice of the photographs, the choice of music and spoken tributes. Kudos! This is a tremendous thing you've done and on behalf of myself, and mine, thank you for caring enough to do it.

HTTP://MEMBERS.HOME.NET/DIANATRIBUTE

Begert's site offers a graphics program that can be downloaded free of charge. It includes the story of Diana's life, photos, and interview film and sound clips. Acknowledging the populist base of cyberspace celebrity devotion, Begert offers a special thanks to "the dozens of people" who contributed material for the program and to "JAM, the Cyber Goddess," for helping him find a "reliable site that would donate the needed space for the program and the web page."

The virtual pilgrimages that Diana's fans make to her mourning sites are an important aspect of the sites' ritualistic value. At Begert's site, guestbook entries provide a poignant record of people's thoughts during their virtual pilgrimage experience. Aly, from Houston, became pensive about how much Diana meant to her:

At first i did not know her but when i started hearing about her i felt something about her in my heart and at that time i was only 10 and know for some reason in my heart i still think she is alive (she is in my heart). i love princess Diana she was beautful charming caring loving I used to pray evrint that god bring her back into this world we need her down here no one can ever replace Princess Diana. . . . Aly

Elyse, from California, wrote:

Im only 12 and i am doing a report on her [Princess Diana].I found out alout of things i didnt know about her like how she was the first person to touch (or hold) a person who had AIDS, and how she touched alout of peoples hearts. Im really sorry that she died she ment alout to this world, and other people

Using all capital letters, Jennifer, of Louisiana, shouted a message to the Diana fans to follow:

DEAR PRINCESS DIANA LOVERS, FIRST OF ALL I WOULD LIKE TO EXPRESS MY DEEPEST PRAYERS TO ALL OF YOU HEART BROKEN PEOPLE IN, "WALES" I KNOW HOW MUCH SHE MEANT TO EACH AND EVERYONE OF YOU. TO ME SHE WAS LIKE A 2ND MOTHER BUT ONLY IN SPIRIT BECAUSE WE BOTH KNEW THAT WE COULD NOT BE THERE WITH EACH OTHER. EVERY YEAR ON THE DAY, "MUMMY" LEFT US I GO IN MY ROOM AND GO TO MY STAND WERE ALL OF MY PICTURES ARE OF HER AND I LIGHT ABOUT 4 CANDLES AND I PRAY THAT, "MUMMY" IS STILL WATCHING OVER ME TO THIS DAY WHICH THIS MORNING I WOKE UP AND ALL OF A SUDDEN I FELT HER ENTER MY HEART AND THERE IS WERE SHE SHALL REMAIN!!!!! I LOVE YOU ALL VERY MUCH, JENNIFER

With her profound belief in Diana, Jennifer unabashedly expressed the celebrity-religionist's central creed. Celebrities are lightning rods to the divine. When the celebrities die, their Websites become the sole remaining outlet for their sacred power.

The Celebrity Altar: Keanu Reeves and the Dudes

A celebrity altar further illuminates the phenomenon of celebrity-based popular religion in cyberspace. One is a site designed to honor the spiritual insights of Keanu Reeves; it is designed by fans who call themselves the Dudes of the Keanic Circle. The high humor the Dudes' exhibit throughout the site is typical of Web altars. Simultaneously promoting and undermining the idea of deity, the Dudes dally with the divine—an approach that has historical precedents in Christianity's Teresa of Avila, Judaism's Kabbalah, and Bhakti Hinduism.

Keanu Reeves burst into youth consciousness in 1989 when he played a feature role in the slapstick comedy film *Bill and Ted's Excellent Adventure.* The major talent Reeves displayed in the film was an ability to emote a goofy optimism. Ted greeted everything that happened with a

vacant grin, yelping, "Excellent!" His irrepressible optimism hit a resonant chord in the youth market. The word *excellent* entered the daily lexicon of the young. Reeves became a star.

In 1996, his fans built a Web altar to him in cyberspace and took their name. The fan altar's welcome page consists of a black background with a circular picture of a teenage Reeves outlined in bright yellow. Soft synthesized organ music plays in the background, reminiscent of the music that precedes many Christian worship services. Underneath the photo of Reeves, the Dudes introduce themselves. They explain the unsystematic nature of the Keanic teachings they have assembled and express a wish that visitors to the site will be as inspired by Keanu as they have been:

Us Dudes are worshippers of the Keanic Light, brought into the world by the one called Keanu Reeves, Enlightened Being, Mighty Roller of the Keanic Wheel, Lord of Lords, and Dude of Dudes. We of the Keanic Circle base our faith upon the Visions of the Dudes who bask in his most excellent Light. It is no cause for concern if some of the Visions seem to contradict each other, for they are all true to the Light. Vision things are like that. We hope that each and every one of you will enter the Keanic Circle and be totally blissed.

HTTP://USERS.AOL.COM/KEANICDUDE/KEANICS.HTM

Farther down the page, the site has a menu of three choices: "Offerings," "Sayings," and "e-mail the dudes." Below the three choices is a disclaimer that insists the site is not sponsored by Keanu Reeves or approved by him. In fact, the Dudes say, Keanu may not even know they exist. Then, in the very next paragraph, they proclaim that, well, yes, he does know they exist; but theirs still is an unofficial site.

On the Offerings page, another photo of Reeves is prominently displayed. Superimposed over it is a light-reflecting helmet with a cross in the position of Reeves's nose and an open doorway over his mouth. An odd caption follows:

Whoops! Dude Alf, while seeking enlightenment, threw up on the printer. Well, we still have 2 more years of welfare as we know it.

HTTP://USERS.AOL.COM/KEANICDUDE/WELFARE.HTM

No means to contribute money is provided; thus, visitors learn, the Dudes are not out for fan money. But the Dudes may, like their idol Reeves, be out to make fans laugh.

The Sayings page opens with a re-creation of Leonardo da Vinci's *Last Supper,* with Reeves's head superimposed on the Christ figure seated at the center of the table. Leonardo's Christ is seated at two other places around the table, implying that the Dudes do not see Reeves so much replacing Christ as superseding him. Underneath the Christ-Reeves painting, the "sayings" of Keanu are posted. Most are scatological riffs on passages from the Christian Bible attributed to Christ:

If someone says to you, "The Dude says thus,"
do not believe it.
The Dude does not say.
••••••••••••••••••

Keanic Wisdom is like a tiny mustard seed
hidden in fifty pounds of dung.
Doesn't sound very tasty, does it?
But the dung dissolves and feeds the seed
until it grows to become a delicious
hot dog garnish.
Let he who has ears listen!

HTTP://USERS.AOL.COM/KEANICDUDE/SAYINGS.HTML

The Clues, or Prophecies, page is the mystical code book of the Keanic Dudes' virtual altar. It describes how one can "read" Keanu's films to gain Keanic wisdom. To the Dudes, each Reeves film contains bits of prophecy. The Dudes' particular forte is their ability to recognize these clues and assemble them meaningfully for the enlightenment of the Keanu faithful:

Clues, or Prophesies, of the coming and significance of Keanu, our Lord and Dude, appear in many of His movies and in other sources. It is one of the tasks of the Dudes to identify and catalogue these clues and present them to the faithful on this very web page, so that the world may know we are not just making this all up.

HTTP://USERS.AOL.COM/KEANICDUDE/CLUES.HTM

The Dudes present links that invite visitors to explore four Reeves films: *Brotherhood of Justice, Bram Stoker's Dracula, Even Cowgirls Get the Blues,* and *Bill and Ted's Excellent Adventure.* On the *Brotherhood of Justice* page, visitors can activate a film clip of a kiss between Reeves and costar Lori Loughlin. To the Dudes, the film's "true" meaning is revealed in a conversation between Christy (Loughlin) and a character named Victor as to what Reeves is really like:

CHRISTY: We've been together for almost two years. I just don't understand Him anymore.
VICTOR: Maybe He's not who you think He is. Maybe He's not who He thinks He is.

To make sure visitors do not fail to pick up on what the Dudes perceive as the transcendent significance of Victor's reply, they add a coda to the conversation.

He is not who you think He is.

HTTP://USERS.AOL.COM/KEANICDUDE/CLUE01.HTM

On the page dedicated to Reeves's appearance in *Bram Stoker's Dracula,* the Dudes include a still from the film in which Reeves holds a candle. In the photo, the candle itself glows. The Dudes insist that the candle glows because it is in contact with Reeves. To the Dudes, the photo demonstrates Reeves's mystical light. Anything he touches can take it on. It is an instance of his spiritual uniqueness caught on film. The text they include with the photo vibrates with fan enthusiasm:

KEANIC LIGHT

This one is easy to miss in the theater, but if you look at this still shot, you can clearly see His Light coming, not from the flame of the candle, but from the candlestick! Coppola didn't even notice this magical escape of Keanic Light! If he had, he would have edited it out so as not to distract from his "story." But the Dudes know the real story.

HTTP://USERS.AOL.COM/KEANICDUDE/CLUE02.HTM

The Dudes employ a similar logic when they set about deciphering the hidden meaning of Reeves's appearance in *Even Cowgirls Get the Blues*. The page boasts an unelaborate design, a large square clip from the movie with Reeves's head floating in the clouds, accompanied by a short explanatory text:

He shall come upon the clouds.

When the Dudes see this movie, they ask, "What is the Light Bringer doing in this turkey, anyway?" He has an asthma attack and appears in the sky as a god. That's it. The Dudes have concluded that the asthmatic episode was merely a comment on the movie, and this scene is the revealing of the godhead. Indude, there is no other explanation.

HTTP://USERS.AOL.COM/KEANICDUDE/CLUE03.HTM

The most enigmatic of the Dudes' prophecy pages purports to decipher the concealed clues embedded in *Bill and Ted's Excellent Adventure*. Multiple photos that take visitors through the film's entire story are accompanied by extensive text explanations. The general introduction sums it up:

SAN DIMAS SAVIORS

This movie totally oozes with clues, and is so central to the Keanic Revelation that it will be dealt with in great detail on a separate page. But, aside from the obvious similarity of the plot to the Dude Most High's role in the real world, there are a couple of clues that single out Keanu. Bill and Ted are first introduced to time travel and to THEMSELVES at the Circle K early on in the movie. Can there be doubt in anyone's mind as to who "K" is? It is none other than Keanu Reeves, the Dude Made Flesh, Conquerer of the Evil One and his Bogus Servants, Avatar of Eternal Light, and Dialectic Destroyer of the World. Praise His name! In Bill and Ted, the Bodacious One also reveals His task to the world. Upon His left thigh it is written, "Save the Humans." And so He shall!

HTTP://USERS.AOL.COM/KEANICDUDE/CLUE04.HTM

Not all celebrity worship involves exaltation. In the case of Keanu Reeves, another Web site takes the opposite tack. Its authors agree with the Dudes that Reeves is more than an actor. Labeled the Keanu Report, this Reeves-slamming site insists that far from being a model of light and goodness, Reeves is instead a manifestation of paramount evil. He is, they contend, the anti-Christ:

The general distaste and antipathy that follows the public life of Keanu Reeves is nothing new. However, few of the people who have opinions on the young man, in favor or against, realize the truth: that Keanu Reeves is the manifestation of evil on Earth, the Anti-Christ.

HTTP://WWW.GEOCITIES.COM/HOLLYWOOD/6608/KEANU.HTML

Since the Dudes have attracted anti-Dudes, one can only wonder whether we will soon be treated to a virtual Keanu Reeves Armageddon.

Celebrity Community: Trekkers in Cyberspace

Although Lady Diana sites in cyberspace are mournfully lovely and the Dudes' Keanic altar is a wickedly clever mimetic of Reeves's breakthrough cinematic persona, both are mere blips on the radar screen of cyberspace when compared to the virtual outpouring of *Star Trek* fans. *Star Trek* sites use the television series of the same name as the organizing principle behind a host of tiny subcommunities that reinforce each other in strongly countercultural behavior by way of a mammoth virtual presence.

A by-product of the shift to mass-mediated global culture has been that the cultural influence of priests, rabbis, and other traditional sources of charismatic authority is being challenged by that of entertainers.

Star Trek fans were a potent force long before the Web came into existence. They took inspirational genesis from *Star Trek*, a television series from the creative genius of Gene Roddenberry. The series aired for three seasons, from fall 1966 through spring 1969. Set in the twenty-second century, the operant theme of the series was exploration of outer space. Story lines revolved around the space travel of the USS *Enterprise,* under the command of Captain James T. Kirk, portrayed with casual offhandedness by William Shatner. The ship's mission, announced in the opening prologue of each episode, was "to explore the galaxy, to seek out new life, and to boldly go where no man has gone before."

Patterned after the Greek hero Ulysses, Captain Kirk was the protagonist of the series. But a handful of supporting characters who made up the nub of the *Enterprise* crew became hugely popular as well. The most prominent ancillary character was Commander Spock (played by Leonard Nimoy). A pointed-eared being from the imaginary planet Vulcan, whose native populace embraced a behavioral standard of stoic and emotionless rationality, Mr. Spock could achieve a Vulcan mind meld with any living creature merely by touching the base and side of its head.

Other central characters were Montgomery Scott, or "Scottie" (played by James Doohan), the ship's chief engineer; Lieutenant Uhura (played by Nichelle Nichols, one of the first African American women to land a featured role in a television series), the ship's communication officer; and Dr. Leonard "Bones" McCoy (DeForest Kelly), the ship's chief medical officer.

Though the TV *Star Trek* produced a corpus of only seventy-nine episodes, the fictional world it sketched attracted the most fervently loyal fans in television history. First known as Trekkies and later Trekkers, *Star Trek* fans stubbornly supported the series long after its demise. They lobbied for the show's return. They organized *Star Trek* conferences. They invested considerable money and effort to create personal *Star Trek* costumes that they wore to conventions, bookstore events, and sometimes their own weddings.

Intrepid fan support eventually attracted new money and energy to the *Star Trek* phenomenon. The second generation included an animated television series, numerous books, six full-length feature films starring many members of the original cast, and three spin-off television series *(Star Trek: The Next Generation, Star Trek: Deep Space Nine,* and *Star Trek: Voyager).*

Through intense commitment to a fictional series and its characters, Trekkers dramatize the extent to which mass-mediated entertainment took on a religious function for part of its audience base at the end of the twentieth century. The central organizing point for *Star Trek* on the Web is the Star Trek Nexus. It greets visitors with a statement of its encompassing nature:

Welcome to Star Trek Nexus, with 48 categories and over 1500 links. If something is NOT accessible from Star Trek Nexus, it probably does not exist.

HTTP://MEMBERS.AOL.COM/TREK.NEWS/INDEX.HTM

Trekker fan sites are international and multilingual. They can be accessed in Portuguese, German, French, Japanese, and Spanish as well as English. There are Trekker sites for youth. There are Trekker sites for gays and lesbians. In the virtual subuniverse of Trekkerdom, a host of fan communities have arisen.

The Website constructed by the oldest continuous *Star Trek* club is a paramount example of a community celebrity site. Its sponsor is the Boston Star Trek Club of America, or BSTA. Like the Dudes, BSTA offers a Web page (http://members.aol.com/bsta1701/bstainfo.html) that introduces itself and its purpose for any visitors who might drop by. An interesting aspect of BSTA's introduction is the list of concrete activities in which the group is engaged. They include a semimonthly newsletter, a monthly BSTA calendar, monthly BSTA meetings, a membership kit, regular BSTA outings, and the IDIC (Infinite Diversity in Infinite Combinations), the club's charity branch.

In contrast to the Dudes, who mimicked and at times mocked the steps of authoritative theological endeavor, the Trekkers of BSTA leave such mimicry behind. On the page identified as the Captain's Log (http://members.aol.com/LinkyS/caplog.html), they guide visitors to fan fiction, known as *fanfic,* published in cyberspace. These stories are not spoofs but serious fictional endeavors springing from the imagination of Trekkers. With themes of love and betrayal, seduction and abandonment, these stories take characters through trials of loneliness, death, and divorce.

Like the Dudes' Sayings, the significance Trekkers attribute to what initially entered our cultural milieu as an entertainment vehicle is difficult for nonfans to take seriously. Does Web-published Trekker fanfic amuse, distract, arouse, inspire? The authors themselves claim they cannot always be sure. Yet the ethic of the Prime Directive, the fictional lives of the characters originally breathed to life by Roddenberry, and the others who followed in their wake, are an imaginative obsession for Trekkers the world over. Some claim they are working out the future for all of humankind through their Trek experiences. If they are right, this virtually promulgated celebrity-based religion could be our religious future.

Online Celebrity Religion and Our Religious Future

For much of the modern period, religion and entertainment occupied distinct cultural spheres. People who excelled in one or the other achieved significant public recognition, but the quality of the recognition differed. The seriousness of people and ideas associated with the religious sphere was rarely called into question. A religious leader modeled or taught what the world was ultimately about and how to live in it. Those who rejected a religious leader's teachings often did so more from dismay at the leader's failure to live in accordance with her or his ideals than from lack of interest or disbelief.

Entertainers were people of a different ilk. A source of amusement or distraction, they were unlikely exemplars of correct or admirable behavior. Although their skills at amusement were highly valued, the virtue of entertainers was customarily impugned.

Mass media eroded the barriers between these spheres of human activity. They made it possible for Lady Diana and Mother Teresa, Keanu Reeves and a fictional Star Fleet commander to appear on the same public "stage." The common appearances had a leveling effect that militated against their differences. Hence a by-product of the shift to mass-mediated global culture has been that the cultural influence of priests, rabbis, and other traditional sources of charismatic authority is being challenged by that of entertainers. Interestingly, celebrity worship has not substantially altered the moral repute of entertainers as objects of fans' interest. The celebrities around whom fans constellate are gods of clay who, possibly because they are of clay and thus breakable and earthy, seem to be close, real, and valuable.

The phenomenon of popular-culture religions was well under way before interactive new media such as the Internet and the World Wide Web were invented. Yet cyberspace is playing an important role in their growth. By offering an ideal environment, a public hothouse in which these fledgling religions can grow, cyberspace enables fans to declare to each other and the world where they have staked out their sacred domains.

Celebrity-based religions exist because people want them and commit themselves to them. Before cyberspace, there was little traditional religionists could do to respond to their rise. It is mildly ironic, then, that the cyberspace public arena amenable to popular religions is also a public arena where traditional religions can finally compete with them. Just as traditional media create a vast stage on which celebrity personalities thrive, the new medium of cyberspace creates a small, compact stage where content is everything. Since constructing and preserving dense meanings is a forte of traditional religion, cyberspace offers a fascinating forum for them to interact with popular religions such as the Keanic Light and Trekkers—quite possibly to the betterment of both sides.

It is ironic that the cyberspace public arena amenable to popular religions is also a public arena where traditional religions can finally compete with them.

For people on the outside, new religions are easy to dismiss. Purportedly an avenue to ultimate meaning, the upstart religions necessarily display the novelty that makes them appear risky and transitory to a noninitiate. Adding a celebrity factor to the mix heightens the effect. But for their part, traditional religions lulled by the achievement of cultural predominance can become mired in the past. Absent any challenge from new religion, an existing religion can stagnate. Thus too quickly marginalizing popular-culture religious groups such as Trekkers may shortchange both a potentially meaningful critique of existing religious traditions and the means by which traditional religions could reveal the cracks in new religious systems as they appear.

The opportunity for open confrontation between traditional and popular religion comes with a subtle challenge attached. Will the better spirituality win? If traditional religion becomes a protected use of cyberspace, we may find out. If not, we had best prepare to hail the celebrity gods online, because their connection to profit in the entertainment industry guarantees that cyberspace celebrity worship will be preserved—albeit heavily patrolled for copyright infringements—even if traditional religious devotion vanishes from the virtual horizon.

Existential Doubt, or Does a Cyborg Have a Soul?

The tools we use are not just aids; they contribute to our definition as a life form.

Whether anything distinguishes us as human beings from other life forms and what, if anything, that could be are religious, philosophical, and biological questions about which few observers agree. Although animals from great apes to anteaters employ simple implements such as sticks to live, only humans use complex tools extensively and for innumerable purposes. The tools we use are not just aids; they contribute to our definition as a life form.

As a new and explosively useful tool, the computer simultaneously reconfigures the content of what we do and redefines precisely who we are. Scholars of cultural studies refer to today's computer-symbiotic variety of human identity as the *cyborg*. This is not to suggest that we are being physically altered by our computerized environment in the Lamarckian sense that the social traits we develop are passed on to our offspring. Rather it suggests that the computer has transformed our dominant patterns of human play, work, love, birth, sickness, and death so much that cyborg is a metaphor we live by. A term of and for our times, cyborg maps contemporary bodily and social reality as a computer-biology hybrid.

> The computer simultaneously reconfigures the content of what we do and redefines precisely who we are.

The advent of online religion may be surprisingly strong in part because it embraces the cyborg aspects of the self that are neglected in traditional religious settings. Online religion privileges the imagination and senses, the ideas and relationships evoked by computer-mediated communication. To the extent this is the case, online religion represents an emergent expression of public values. Its rituals and communities, its theologies and images are the outgrowth of a widespread human effort to come to terms with the changes computers induce within as well as among us. Online religion represents the early effort of a rapidly computerized humanity to spiritualize a novel habitus. Like mounting a mezuzah on the doorpost or a crucifix in the living room of a new abode, online religion classifies cyberspace as a valued and value-producing home.

The impact the computer is having on human identity has serious implications for traditional religion. The computer introduces to the palette of human experience cyberspace, virtual communities, and a host of other computer-reliant phenomena that fall outside the corpus of our inherited religious ideas and stories. For religiously inclined or committed people, a computer-informed, globally networked worldview can make some inherited religious goods appear insufficiently comprehensive and therefore less credible, less persuasive, and (at the most practical level) less useful.

This is quite noticeably true for those attached to traditions such as Reform Judaism and liberal Protestantism that encourage an open-eyed encounter with the modern world. But a computer-infused worldview can also be corrosive to those forms of religious fundamentalism intentionally founded in reaction to modernity. For instance, Christian fundamentalist leaders, avid practitioners of online religion though they be (see Chapter Eight), consider a freely accessible cyberspace dangerous to their belief system. They have been at the forefront of the campaign to develop and proliferate software filters that can limit the range of individual cyberspace involvement.

One of my favorite Web cartoons uses humor to draw attention to the challenge cyberspace poses to fundamental theology's conventional idea of God. The drawing shows a white-robed, white-bearded, traditional-looking God figure, sitting slump-shouldered at a computer terminal. His head is turned such that he looks morosely out at the reader. Beneath the drawing, the caption reads, "On the Web, nobody knows that you are God."

The humor of this cartoon springs from the tensions inherent in two ideas. The first is the notion that a traditional deity could become so intrigued by CMC that he or she could not resist going online. By itself, the idea stirs up a small chuckle and brings low-grade humor into play. However, the real punch from the cartoon derives from the second idea it slips in: once online, such a traditional God would be frustrated to learn that what humanity had deemed his or her most important aspect—unique divinity—was completely incommunicable in the virtual environment. This is the cartoon's potent punch line, because in cyberspace no one can really know that you are God (that is, if you are a conventional God) because unequivocal, unique identities are not possible.

Historically, religions have been the paramount cultural organizations that generate understanding of what it means to be human. Every major world religion possesses a belief system that explains what it means to be human and what the ultimate status of the human being is in the wider universe. Yet oddly enough, traditional religious thinkers have remained fairly silent about the computer revolution. An eclectic combination of writers and artists—canaries in the cave of cyberspace—have not. They have written or dramatized or sculpted their ideas about how computerization alters what it means to be human. Their symbols and myths constitute the first generation of cyberspace theology, providing a series of sizzling cultural vehicles through which the implications of cyberspace for human identity and the import of online religion can be explored.

How We Became Cyborg

To understand how we became cyborg, we must start with awareness of the profound dependence on others that marks all human life. Years ago, social constructivists Peter Berger and Thomas Luckmann detailed the dialectical processes at work in human identity construction.[1] As lucid as their analysis was, it really only delineated what life experiences teach everyone: becoming human is a social endeavor. People determine who they are through interaction with the environments they encounter; in turn, they shape those environments by their action and inaction with and toward them. If you were born to Mormon parents in Salt Lake City, you are more likely than not as an adult to be an American citizen who speaks English and attends a Latter-day Saints church.

At one company, office employees who had previously worked well as a team lost the habit of talking with their neighbors after computerization was introduced.

Crossing the threshold of the third millennium, computers profoundly structure social life in the West. Computers begin with artifacts, but the computerization of humanity is more than an amassing of those artifacts. It is in fact a culture. It makes up a "signifying system through which . . . social order is communicated, reproduced, experienced and explored."[2] Computers are also an epistemology or way of knowing, in which new computers or new software materializes as the most plausible response to whatever problems arise. Computers yield social relationships that require production, distribution, and consumption of computer goods and services to survive. A flagrant result of this technological saturation is that people are being transformed into cyborgs: partly imaginative, partly real creatures evoked into existence through human-computer semiotics. From automated traffic lights to cookie-triggered advertising, from standardized testing to automated banking, the computer is homogenizing the human. Day by day, we become more and more cyborg.

Though some people cannot afford or care not to invest in modern technology's seductive computer products, no one evades cyborgian symptoms. Because it calls attention to the tremendous impact computers are having on us, the cyborg has become a key interpretive symbol for the contemporary human self. Like the words *vassal, lord, citizen,* and *proletarian* before it, the word *cyborg* paints humanness in a historical context. It discloses how the organization of contemporary social and political life is working in consort with computers as the reigning means of production to influence the range of humanness possible in our era.

Cyber-punk simultaneously developed as a science fiction subgenre and an outlaw youth identity that gloried in postmodern identification of humans with computers. However, the confusion of boundaries that exhilarated cyber-punk fans brought severe distress to others. The research of sociologist Shoshana Zuboff on the effect of computerization on office environments disclosed how introducing technological developments meant to expand worker skills can cause worker sociability to implode.[3] At one company Zuboff studied, office employees who had pre-

viously worked well as a team abandoned their customary sociability once computers were introduced. Compelled to develop work patterns that centered on computers, the office workers carried on this independence of action even when it was not useful. After computerization, whenever problems arose, people would strive to resolve them individually rather than ask the person sitting in the cubicle next to them for help. They lost the habit of talking with their neighbors.

Although I characterize technology's role in human socialization as massive, I do not mean to imply that all cyborgs are identical. Demographic factors constrain the presence and composition of the mix of biology and computer, while widespread resource imbalances serve up divergent experiences of cyborg socialization across the globe. Consider CMC. Cyborg experiences on the World Wide Web can be exhilarating. One can tour the Vatican museum, order airline tickets, or research aboriginal tribes all without leaving one's chair. The fusion with technology that yields this techno-marvel can seem a wondrous thing.

But these experiences are available only to those who have access to a computer with a modem hooked into an available telephone or cable line and who have enough computer savvy to put everything together and make it work. Billions do not possess these resources; global biases are evident in their unequal distribution. In many parts of the world, most notably in the Southern Hemisphere, the existing infrastructure simply does not support the spread of CMC. In Peru, there is one telephone line for every thirty people; in southern Africa, one line for every five thousand. In locations where the public infrastructure is so limited, very few readily surf the Net.

To privileged first-worlders, cyborg identity can bring with it an explosion of the self, an expansion of the human beyond precyborgian limits. Individuals and families can develop a homepage that contains their own self-constructed myths. Videotelephoning on the Internet brings the images and voices of far-off loved ones into your home. Newspapers and even books can be downloaded free of charge. Excerpts from the latest CD recording, film clips, and news overviews are all a few keystrokes away. But to the less privileged, becoming "borged" too often means having one's humanity annexed by a computer.

Theology in Strange Places: Hel and Hiro as Religious Parables

Although traditional religionists rarely analyze or critique the cyborg, science fiction authors and filmmakers tackle the topic with glee. In science fiction films and novels, cyborgs are technological golems; they mimic human life but remain outside it. A veritable spectrum of cyborgs have flittered through the products of mass entertainment in recent decades, generating some of its most memorable images. They include the human illusions manufactured by aliens in *The Matrix,* the Nexus 6 replicants in *Blade Runner,* and Data, the android who longs to be human, in *Star Trek: The Next Generation.* Amid the narratives through which they saunter, these fictional cyborgs serve as a counterpoint to humanness, which, by contrast, reveals that being fully human is a desirable (or, more rarely, an undesirable) trait. In the process, cyborg narratives raise essential religious questions about whether and how it is possible to discern a boundary between humanness and computer technology.

Cyborg narratives raise essential religious questions about whether and how it is possible to discern a boundary between humanness and computer technology.

In film, the genesis of the cyborg can be traced to 1926, a year before the medium saw its first talking film. It was linked to cultural reactions against the mass routinization of labor ushered in by World War I. In the

United States, religious reactions to the devastation of the war ranged from the social gospel of Protestant theologian Walter Rauschenbusch to the rise of a militant, antimodernist movement later to be known as Christian fundamentalism. But the arts produced powerful responses as well. Less than two decades after the first Ford Model T was sold, a startlingly futuristic, female-appearing robot named Hel eerily materialized on the screen in Fritz Lang's *Metropolis*.

Aptly foreshadowing the computerized future, Lang visually presented the cyborg as an explicit synthesis of the mechanical and the human. At first an awkward-moving, metal-skinned machine, Hel received a transfusion of blood involuntarily removed from a saintlike but very human woman named Maria. As fluid drawn from Maria flooded Hel's metallic structure, Hel was transformed into the first screen cyborg.

Hel becomes a defective copy of Maria and proceeds to wreak havoc on the city of Metropolis. Director Lang made no attempt to use Hel's mimicking of Maria's countenance to throw the audience into a state of confusion between the two. Instead, he presented the entire transformation process and then cut back and forth between the transformed Hel and the weakened Maria, forcing viewers to remain constantly aware that Hel was not human but a hybrid of humanity and technology. Given Hel's subsequent destructiveness and the Luddite philosophy that drives the plot (a philosophy quietly undermined by the technological medium and artistry of the film itself), the evil resonances of Hel's name cannot be dismissed as coincidence. Though humanity in Metropolis is far from perfect, Hel (Hell) is a cyborg.

Three-quarters of a century later, Neal Stephenson's science fiction novel *Snow Crash* appeared,[4] at a time when global computerization was becoming a reality. It deals directly with the pernicious effects of computerized humanity. The novel's main story revolves around an elite cadre

of Net specialists who are out for hire as virus fighters, connecting directly to the Internet via bodily implants. Bypassing skin and other bodily
sensual input systems, their implanted electronic jacks make it possible
for them to experience a completely fused mental-sensual life. The wear-
ers of these jacks live in a state of experiential directness that far exceeds
anything a noncomputerized body can deliver.

In *Snow Crash,* Hiro Protagonist is the best Net cowboy around. He
waltzes in cyberspace with a velvet grace that could put a virtual Fred
Astaire to shame. When Hiro runs afoul of his employer, the employer
knows exactly what to do to punish him: he has Hiro's implants brutally
stripped from his body. The loss of his technologically mediated sensual-
ity leaves Hiro bereft.

Attempting to relate to the concrete world directly through his bodily senses, Hiro finds it uninspiringly flat and dull. As a sensory input
organism, his unaugmented body cannot match the brain jazz that his
cyborg body delivered with ease. To Hiro, bodily life becomes an unbear-
able disappointment. His biological frame is simply "the meat"—the
muscles, fat, and bone that make the ecstasy of cybernetic life possible.
Aching for the direct stimuli of the jacks, Hiro caves in to the torture that
normal sensual life has become. He agrees to do whatever his boss wants,
to get the jacks back. Unreflective acceptance of technological advances
makes Hiro no hero but rather a being cruelly addicted to the technology
he thinks exists to please and serve him.

The History of the Cyborg

As Lang's work illustrates, fictional admixtures of human and technological lumbered about in the realm of the aesthetic long before computer
technology existed. They were employed by artists as metaphors to
explore humanity's uneasy relationship with its own technology. The term

cyborg first appeared in 1960, in a speculative article on the future of space travel written by two research scientists, Manfred Clynes and Nathan Kline.[5] Rather than developing human-friendly environments for space travel, Clynes and Kline made the unorthodox proposal that scientists try to alter the human body so it can thrive in space. They referred to these space-adapted humans as "cyborgs."

Shortly afterward, cultural critics picked up the term and started using it as a metaphor through which to discuss how increasingly difficult it was to perceive boundaries between the human and the technological artifice. Though the French semiologist Roland Barthes never explicitly uses the word *cyborg,* his provocative writings fall into this category. Barthes culturally decoded Albert Einstein as a kind of natural cyborg in early 1957.[6] He claimed that Einstein was too intellectual to fit comfortably within the normal range of humanness; hence he was dismembered in the popular imagination to become signified by his brain. In this detached state, Einstein's brain was culturally venerated as a remarkable computerized object, a marvelous human machine (ergo, a cyborg). To the public, Einstein's cyborg brain produced novel thought "as a mill makes flour."

Furthering the linguistic transformation of the cyborg from a biological term to a metaphor of cultural semiotics, scholars enthusiastically began to write about the cyborg as a cardinal symbol of the late-twentieth-century, postindustrial world. The scholar who achieved the greatest notoriety in this regard was historian of science Donna J. Haraway. In the 1980s, Haraway laid out a thorough framework of the cultural cyborg concept in her now renowned "cyborg manifesto."[7] A pivotal article in cyborg deliberations, Haraway's manifesto detailed many of the acute ethical issues modern technology induces, including the militarization of human imagination by new media technologies. In spite of the problems she foresaw, Haraway ultimately took a stand endorsing the influence of technology on human life. She insisted that cyborg imagery offered "a way out of the maze of dualisms in which we have explained our bodies and our tools to

Give Me That Online Religion

ourselves."[8] In a move that simultaneously anticipated and ignored poststructuralist concerns, Haraway not only invoked the cyborg in her analysis but also overtly and playfully celebrated its existence.

Another who, like Barthes, never employed the term yet whose work offered an important, early contribution to cyborg discourse was feminist theologian Naomi Goldenberg. Five years after Haraway's cyborg-celebratory "Manifesto," Goldenberg offered a substantially gloomier prognosis of the cyborg based on what she perceived to be the psychological implications of human-machine interdependence.[9] Contra Haraway, Goldenberg decried the enlarging role of machines—especially computers—in human  socialization. The philosophical and religious heritage of the West, Goldenberg claimed, leaves Westerners predisposed to form harmful attitudes toward the technologies overtaking their lives. This heritage has taught us "that human life is a rough copy of something out there—something better, wiser and purer. . . . "[10] Westerners possess a cultural proclivity to respond to machines not as tools for use but as role models for emulation. As people act on this impulse, the isolation and loneliness of modern life increase. Given the protechnology bent of Western development, Goldenberg's prediction for the future is a somber one: "We are, I think, engaged in a process of making one another disappear by living more and more of our lives apart from other humans, in the company of machines."[11]

It is precisely because of all this that the cyborg, a metaphor through which the character of contemporary humanity is being deliberated, is of great consequence for the future of religion. As Stephenson's Hiro character facilely demonstrates, the textures and smells, tastes and touches associated with nonaugmented human life quickly take on a negative value for those who imaginatively exist in the quasi-virtuality of cyberspace, simultaneously enmeshing cyborgs in the material world. The pattern of human identities this semi-imaginative dimension encourages are considerably at odds with the theological anthropology of traditional, life-affirming religions such as Judaism, Christianity, and Islam, as well as the material-rejecting theological anthropology sponsored by traditions such as Buddhism and Hinduism. Yet in the cyborg debates, religious leaders and academic theologians have largely been silent in the face of this vital challenge to much of their core beliefs, opting to go along with the process (at least as far as maintaining a Web presence).

Biblical Religions and the Cyborg

For the biblical religions of Judaism, Christianity, and Islam, cyborg identities pose a subtly comprehensive challenge. A notable measure of the internal cohesion of the world's major religions derives from biblical texts, which set out guidelines for human-to-human relationships and human relationships to the divine. The stories and ideas in biblical writings originated among pastoralist and agrarian peoples. The religious messages they convey assume as a given that human existence is embodied existence. But for cyborgs, universal embodiment is not the defining situation. Instead, it is a preeminent moral question, as selves ambiguously colonized by technological tools confront unique border quandaries such as the techno-blurred boundaries of life and death. For traditional religions, with their links to agrarian and pastoralist origins, to be able to address these concerns, changes may need to occur within their symbol systems—changes that it may be beyond their capacity to make.

Christianity, the most prevalent religion in the United states, poignantly illustrates this dilemma. A focal idea of Christianity is incarnational theology. In all of its diverse manifestations, Christianity pivots around the idea of the embodiment of the divine in human form; however, this notion is problematized by the coupling, now under way, of human and machine.

Ian Barbour, the American theologian who has made the most serious attempt to draw from Christian tradition ethical guidance for contemporary technological society, ends up offering an excellent appraisal of the problem but little normative counsel. He chiefly recommends reading biblical literature through the lens of process theology, to glean from its stories of small communities that survived countless crises how to survive our own. Yet Barbour has no explanation of how reading these stories accomplishes what he himself diagnoses as the critical problem: "to redirect technology to realize human and environmental values."[12]

Christianity pivots around the idea of the embodiment of the divine in human form; however, this notion is problematized by the coupling, now under way, of human and machine.

Though Barbour submits that Christianity possesses religious resources sufficient to address the ethical quandaries of a technological society, he does not exhibit them. He also concedes that churches as Christian delivery systems are woefully unprepared to carry out the tasks his ethical assessment prescribes. In Barbour's words, "The churches, themselves, will have to change drastically if they are to facilitate the transition to a sustainable world."[13]

Technological socialization places theological and sociological obstacles before Barbour that hinder his ability as a religious ethicist to construct a viable, persuasive Christian moral response to technologically derived dilemmas. He must respond to the problems of the modern world using the resources of a symbolic pool stocked with agrarian-based images and stories, and he has to turn subsequently to religious congregations nurtured by the contents of this same pool to support any moral vision he manages to forge. Many theologians are ill disposed to wrestle with technological-cultural issues as a congregational activity precisely because their religious imaginations were shaped in response to tales with agrarian and pastoral roots. This same quandary hampers the ability of traditional religionists to contribute to developing technological ethics throughout the world.

Since it is a coalescence of humans and technology that invokes cyborg identities, progress in religious ethics may require that some key traditional religious ideas be completely reconceived. To put it metaphorically, technological society poses an important question to Christian foundational theology: If a cyber-savior logged on and opted to echo Jesus (in Matthew 8:29) by querying the members of a listserv regarding their understanding of the cyber-savior's being, would the question this savior asked be "Who or what do you say I am?" To paraphrase Yeats, the fearful question of the day for biblical religionists is "What virtual creature from cyberspace slouches toward Bethlehem to be born?"

In the United States, traditional religions are largely techno-avoidant. Still, a small number of the adherents of the world's traditional religions have plunged into new technologies with enthusiasm. In the rapidly growing environment of CMC, one can find Orthodox Jewish Lubavitchers in cyberspace, weekly classes in Buddhism meditation, and the Al Zafa Matrimonial Service for Muslims. There are Web pages for the Vatican, the Union of Orthodox Rabbis, the Christian Church (Disciples of Christ), United Church of Christ, Moravians, Jehovah's Witnesses, Church

> Many theologians are ill disposed to wrestle with technological-cultural issues as a congregational activity precisely because their religious imaginations were shaped in response to tales with agrarian and pastoral roots.

of the Nazarene, and so on. There are countless traditional religious discussion lists, ranging from a group reading Calvin's *Institutes* to interfaith prayer groups.

Still, this techno-maintained spirituality does not transform a traditional religious community into a cyborgian congregation. These efforts mainly imitate real-life events rather than reconfigure them. On the Net, it is new religious movements untethered from ancient texts that appear most at home. Synthesizing multidimensional, real-time rituals, neo-pagan cyborg ritualists play in the medium they inhabit.

The extent to which technological socialization habitually distances cyborgs from traditional religious institutions is not a universal given. The understanding of religion that people acknowledge is an important determinant as well. A strict Barthian Christian or a traditional Muslim might dismiss the influence of technology as religiously irrelevant. Or it might be seen as a concern affecting only the means by which one conveys to a proto-believer the sacred Words, which are assumed unchangeable in content and meaning. However, for those who bracket religion's substantive character to concentrate on the serious cultural role that religious institutions have customarily filled, the challenge of technology is not so easily dismissed.

Taking a stand in significant agreement with Barbour, theologian Gregor Goethals asserts that traditional religious institutions should learn to use new technologies to convey their messages, while at the same time keeping "a prophetic watch over the making of meaning by the media."[14] By this, Goethals suggests that a sanguine response to computer socialization is possible. Much like Barbour, though, Goethals's prognosis regarding the amenability of traditional religionists to following through on such a program is equivocal. According to Goethals, the believers who make up the delivery system of traditional religions "may have little or no desire to take on either task."[15]

A primary cultural function of religious institutions is to respond to the existential questions of their age, or so the twentieth-century Lutheran theologian and cultural critic Paul Tillich would have it. Or the cultural role of religious institutions may be, as world-renowned anthropologist Clifford Geertz contends, to proffer a symbol system that welds together a description of the world and prescriptions for action within it. Either way, technologizing daily life appears to undermine the ability of religious institutions to fulfill these cultural functions. Moving into the cultural space they are vacating (just as *Metropolis* insinuated in its day) are thriving and vibrant popular culture religions.

†The Cyborg's Attraction for Popular-Culture Religion⊥

Overt religions have either inadequately constructed or left unconstructed any timely moral response to the intricate changes in human identity and community induced by computers. Cultural dread and excitement over the transformation of people into cyborgs has exhibited a postmodern independence from frameworks, surfacing not in techno-avoidant or techno-manipulative religious groups but in multiple locations in the techno-celebratory popular culture. Consequently, an undetermined number of cyborgs have turned from what the late French theorist Jean-Paul Baudrillard once cynically described as "the desert of the real"[16] (in this case, the symbolic goods of real-life religious groups) to the "hyper-real," to locate meaning resources sufficient to respond to technology's incursion into their lives. As their concerns about techno-life are ignored or shunted from overtly religious realms, an unknown number of modern technologically socialized people are practicing religion by creatively reusing the artifacts of contemporary mass-mediated culture. These cyborgs find solace for their modernity-driven nightmares in the images, stories, and songs of cable and broadcast television, radio, 'zines, and other alternative media, not in the metaphysical meaning offerings of conventional religious institutions.

This phenomenon has not gone unnoticed. A number of literary, film, and cultural theorists have tackled the topic of the excess-meaning function of popular culture. Yet perhaps because few who have taken up this work are scholars of religion, scant attention has been given to the implications of this development for the historic cultural role of religions. Some hints of its impact can be gleaned from the marginal comments of cultural critics such as Hugh Ruppersberg, who observes, with thinly veiled disapproval, that today's extraterrestrial films are the contemporary equivalent of Bible stories and that the aliens they feature are modern-day messiahs.[17]

> **Cyborgs find solace for their modernity-driven nightmares in the images, stories, and songs of cable and broadcast television, radio, 'zines, and other alternative media.**

At other times, the impact must be surmised, as in the work of literary theorist Janice Radway, who depicts how bold romance heroines inspire some female fans to negotiate less patriarchal bargains with their spouses.[18] Occasionally, a straightforward assessment of the religious function of popular culture has been made, as with historian Peter Brooks's argument that melodrama provides the emotional excesses necessary to help its audiences make moral and ethical decisions in a post-sacred age.[19]

Online religion belies Brooks's contention that our era should be known as the postsacred. The outpouring of energy, time, and innovation—and cash—that makes online religion possible attests to the fact that a good number of people who are fully aware of what modernity has to offer continue to long for the sacred, seeking it out wherever they happen to be. That they do so testifies to stubborn refusal on the part of humanity to let God or the gods go. We may not know exactly how to sacralize cyberspace or what it means to be a virtual sacred self, but a huge number of people are trying to find out. Perhaps some will succeed.

Postscript on the Cyborg

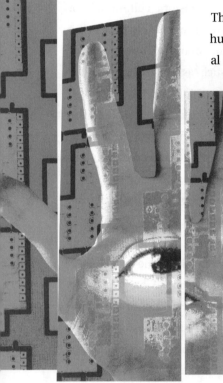

Through its expanding influence on what it means to be human, the computer is inhibiting the ability of traditional religions to reliably inform human self-understanding.

Because their practitioners are acutely aware of the computer's influence on us as individuals and as a society, online traditional and new religions are developing ideas, rituals, and forms of community that assuage this spiritual gap. In short, online religion is a public, communal endeavor to spiritualize cyberspace as humanity's latest abode.

Science fiction films and novels have contributed quite significantly to the ideas undergirding this effort to think through and sacralize the aftereffects of computerization. They have fed a movement toward popular-culture religion that is itself rapidly being taken online. Rather than their traditional counterparts, it is eclectic and homemade religions that have most actively redressed people's fears about the effects computers and computerization are having on them (see Chapter Six). Together, the many facets of online religion play a valuable role in helping us think critically about, and relate to, our technologically sustained environment during an era of significant change.

To the degree that thinking of ourselves as cyborgs reliably orients us in this highly computerized world we inhabit, it can be considered a positive change. There are other benefits as well. As Haraway noted, the cyborg is inherently pluralistic.[20] Rather than employing the fundamental Western dualistic strategy of identifying one thing by contrasting it with another in a hierarchical combination of paired terms (male-female, human-beast, self-other, white-black), the cyborg incorporates dualism within itself. It insists on an integral identity between the material environment and ourselves. The cyborg therefore makes the metaphoric platform of our self-understanding one that encourages complex, relational human identities. The connective links among cyborgs, if they can hold, could stretch out into a net like the World Wide Web itself, bringing us into responsible awareness of and interaction with each other as well as the material world. Online religion points the way.

Virtual Prophets, Instant Global Access, and the Apocalypse

To some modernists, beliefs in supranatural events . . . are needlessly surviving wisps of primitive thought that the products of technological savvy such as the Internet should banish.

An apocalypse is a revelation. In the technical lexicon of biblical studies, *apocalypse* refers to writings that purport to convey a revelation from God. This academic definition stands in considerable contrast to the dominant popular understanding of *apocalypse*. Heavily influenced by Christian storytelling, *apocalypse* in popular use equates to the end of days, when, according to one Christian scenario, the history of the world terminates with a battle at Armageddon (an actual Israeli valley, now known as Megiddo).

In either case, an apocalyptic message typically comes in three parts. It opens with the proclamation that divine judgment is imminent. It insists that this judgment will unleash a cataclysmic transformation of the earth and end human history. It urges a course of action that could forestall the process; "The end is near. Repent!" is a prototypical apocalyptic aphorism.

To some modernists, beliefs in supranatural events such as revelation or apocalypse and universal judgment by a divine power are vestigial religious concepts. They are needlessly surviving wisps of primitive thought that the products of technological savvy such as the Internet should banish. But to the utter dismay of wishful modernists, quite the opposite has occurred. Apocalypticists, so-called doomsday prophets, and other like-minded religious visionaries have taken to the Internet with glee. They happily employ the futuristic technological products of contemporary rationalism to champion ideas that—in rationalists' eyes—erode the underpinnings of rationalist thought.

Evaluating the public import of online religion is woefully incomplete if it omits the involvement of apocalyptic prophets in cyberspace. If the doors to cyberspace remain open for online religion, then it is not just congregations such as a United Methodist Church, a Young Israel synagogue, or a St. Michael's parish that will populate the virtual universe. Alongside them will be Websites extolling the end of the world, crafted by representatives of explicitly apocalyptic movements who include Marshall Applewhite of Heaven's Gate, Marian visionary Veronica Lueken, and evangelical Christian end-times prophet Jack Van Impe.

Countless incidents confirm that apocalyptic patience can run out. Though it is agonizingly difficult to assess the likelihood of the event occurring at any particular time, people under the sway of the apocalyptic can tire of waiting for the ultimate end. In the history of the apocalyptic, some became so frustrated by a God who tarried that they engaged in radical action, hoping to quick-start the divine. In 1969, Australian Denis Michael Rohan set fire to the al-Aqsa mosque in Jerusalem, expecting to hasten Jesus' return.[1] The sarin nerve gas assaults by Aum Shin Rikyo in the Tokyo subway system in 1995 was a trial effort meant to prime the pump of end-times action.[2] The appalling mass murders and suicides of the Restoration of the Ten Commandments of God in 2000 in Uganda eradicated those who might have complained about failed prophecy when a favored leader's prediction of the end failed to materialize.[3]

With the advent of weapons capable of wiping out all planetary life, new social dangers became associated with the persistent apocalyptic tradition. To certain Christian fundamentalists, the atomic bomb—for all its horror—was significant chiefly because it brought about the material means to end the world. Hence they hailed it as the technology of the apocalypse. A brutal fact of today's technologically sophisticated society is that a cabal of two or three parties intent on violence can, with worrisome ease, inflict extensive loss of life and property damage, as the bombing of the Oklahoma City federal government building disastrously proved. Hence the circulation of apocalyptic stories and beliefs in cyberspace imposes a modicum of increased risk to physical security, at least to the extent that it makes widespread violence more imaginable and therefore more inclined to take place. Yet suppressing apocalyptic impulses introduces alternative risks that also must be taken into account.

Because cyberspace is global territory, risk taking can embroil everyone.

Apocalypticism in cyberspace represents a paramount case study in the formidable task of circumscribing the boundaries of global public self-expression for the third millennium. How much risk and what kind of risk people bear with regard to religious expression in modern civil society is generally determined at the political level of the nation-state. Because cyberspace is global territory, risk taking can embroil everyone. So in terms of the relationship between states and religion, it breaks new cultural ground as a backdrop for the apocalyptic, a narrative tradition about the ultimate fate of everyone.

Cyberspace and the Apocalyptic Tradition

Socially speaking, a lone individual who proclaims that the end of the world is near is of relatively minor importance. In cities throughout the United States, end-times prophets appear intermittently, only to vanish after a few weeks or months without a trace. Apocalyptic prophets become socially significant only if and when people hear their message and respond to it with belief and support. Waves of apocalyptic enthusiasm unveil dreams of cosmic finitude on the part of the public, along with those of its leading prophet.

Aflame with apocalyptic enthusiasm, people perceive nearly everything as a cryptic sign that the end of days will soon be upon us. Historian Richard Landes was the first person I ever heard use what became my favorite description of this psychological state.[4] He characterized it as "semiotic arousal," a delightfully apt phrase that captures both the sign-projection dimension and the emotional urgency associated with a bout of apocalyptic fever.

When events threaten to interrupt the unfolding of their end-times vision, the semiotic arousal of apocalypticism can leave people willing to engage in provocative and even violent action.

Attempting to teach a bright undergraduate student about this critical phase of the apocalyptic, I got help one day from nature. Elis, a sophomore majoring in religion, arrived at my office early to walk with me to class. It had been raining heavily for hours. Shortly before we left, the rain stopped. In the middle of the office parking lot, a duck and a swan stood next to each other, nibbling insects that floated in a large rain puddle. Saying a silent prayer of thanks for a great teaching opportunity, I pointed at the birds and exclaimed, with exaggerated urgency, "Ducks and swans standing in parking lots eating together! It's a sign of the end." The reaction on Elis's face told me she got it. Once the apocalyptic lever is tripped in the human mind, almost any random event can become fodder for the widening maw of end-times significance.

Apocalyptic true believers are feverishly active. After all, the immediate present offers the last opportunity to get ready for the colossal changes to come. When they can act according to the rhythms of their beliefs, apocalyptic enthusiasts are inclined to be extremely sweet and generous people. But when events threaten to interrupt the unfolding of their end-times vision, the semiotic arousal of apocalypticism can leave people willing to engage in provocative and even violent action.

Throughout human history, outbreaks of apocalyptic enthusiasm have correlated with myriad factors:

⌘ Unusual social incidents that are interpreted as a "sign of the end times"—perhaps the onset or fading of a powerful symbol. This can include a significant date (although a key symptom of end-times mania is the manufacture of significant dates).

⌘ Rare astronomical events, such as the extraordinarily vivid appearance of a comet or an eclipse.

⌘ Activities or events that threaten the continuation of a religious group, such as unusual external or internal pressures on or within it.

⌘ Major social upheaval, particularly in the area of gender or economics.

Regarding this last point, in the case of gender, rapid liberalization or repression of the prevailing norms in the social organization of sexual differences may spark apocalyptic ferment. In the realm of economic well-being, a rapid swing between extremes of deprivation and affluence is most conducive to apocalyptic currents.

Whereas any one of these events may trigger an isolated outbreak of apocalyptic enthusiasm in a society, a combination of them can impel its spread throughout a society and stimulate an apocalyptic epidemic.

Before widespread mass transportation and mass communication, apocalyptic messages, for all their inherent urgency, could take decades to disseminate. Today, thanks to the World Wide Web, they can be global news in an instant. Not surprisingly, the Netcasting of end-times prophetic pronouncements has become standard practice for apocalyptic groups. There is no question that the Internet furthers the spread of apocalyptic messages. Given how necessary the capacity to attract an audience is to the viability of the apocalyptic, this spread may be a valid cause for concern only during periods when the apocalyptic potential among the populace is high—as when two or more of the historical preconditions prevail.

Only rarely do contemporary apocalyptic groups fail to use the Internet as a vehicle to promulgate their beliefs; but it does happen. Two of the most notorious apocalyptic groups at the turn of the millennium employed little or no Web participation: the Concerned Christians and the Restoration of the Ten Commandments of God (RTCG).

When the presence in Jerusalem of the Colorado apocalyptic group Concerned Christians drew world attention in the fall of 1998, journalists were shocked to learn that the group did not have a Website. "How can any self-respecting apocalyptic group not be on the Web?" leading Israeli journalist Gershom Gorenberg exclaimed.[5] (By the end of 1999, the Concerned Christians did have a Website, albeit one with scant content.)

Uganda presented the second major case of a post-Internet, Web-less apocalyptic. The nightmare of mass death by members of the RTCG unfortunately proved no dream, but law enforcement officials, academics, and journalists searched in vain for a Website belonging to the group.

†The First Internet Tragedy: Heaven's Gate ⊥

One fatal outbreak of apocalyptic enthusiasm in the late twentieth century was definitely linked to Internet use. This was the apocalyptic cocktail of Heaven's Gate (HG). Members of this unaffiliated religious group dwelt in a small mansion in Rancho Santa Fe, California, supporting themselves through the group's Web design company, called Higher Source. In terms of the landscape of American religious life, HG was a small, relatively unknown apocalyptic group. After canvassing the United States by car for decades, advertising in *USA Today,* and mounting an active cyberspace recruitment campaign, HG attracted no more than a hundred members at its peak.

But it garnered international attention on March 25, 1997, when thirty-nine members of the group were found dead. Investigators determined that HG members had killed themselves in a three-day-long death ritual. In stages, group members packed their bags, put a form of personal identification in one pocket and a $5 bill in another, lay down on bunk beds, ate poison-laced food, tied plastic bags over their heads, and died. During each stage but the last, some remained alive to remove the plastic bags from the dead and cover the upper torso of each who died with a purple cloth—ensuring that in death all looked exactly alike.[6]

Images of the HG dead saturated the media for days: body after body stretched out on bunk beds, clad in black pants and black Nike athletic shoes, their faces and chests covered with a purple shroud, each with a neatly packed bag at their side. As news spread about the group's demise, the question most often asked was "Why did they do it?" Given the complex motives that may lie behind so basic an act as telephoning one's mother, any comprehensive summation of HG's motives necessarily remains elusive. Yet apocalypticism was profoundly implicated in the group's violent end, and cyberspace was the principal stage on which that end was dramatized. Under the semiotic arousal of end-times beliefs, HG leaders used the Internet, mass-mediated entertainment, and Christian tradition to develop a fatally flawed architecture of apocalyptic vision. The content of the vision ultimately lured them to enact a ritual of communal death.

At the end of HG's existence, the group relied almost exclusively on the Web to communicate its story. But Heaven's Gate did not start in cyberspace. It began in the 1970s, led by Marshall H. Applewhite and Bonnie Lu Trusdale Nettles, who called themselves, at various times, Bo and Peep, "the Two," "the Him and the Her," and "Do and Ti."

For years, Nettles and Applewhite traveled throughout the United States, recruiting followers. They claimed to hail from another level of reality that they alternately referred to as the Kingdom of Heaven, the Next Level, or the Evolutionary Level Above Human (TELAH). To all who listened, they stated that they had arrived on Earth via a spaceship in the

1970s. Reports of UFO crashes during that period were the material evidence of their arrival, they explained. Ti and Do said they incarnated into human bodies once they arrived, using them as human vehicles to study the earth.[7]

The two rooted Heaven's Gate beliefs in Christian tradition by claiming that Jesus of Nazareth was one of them—a being from TELAH. According to standard HG lore, Ti and Do claimed they were sent from the same kingdom as Jesus by the same Father to tell the same truth (HG "First Statement of Ti and Do," 1–2).[8] Later, Do wrote that he was Jesus, who had returned with his Father (the latter in the body of Ti). Do claimed he had come to earth approximately two thousand years ago and incarnated himself into Jesus' body just prior to the baptism by John. His Father was an "Older Member" from the Kingdom of Heaven who had accompanied him on this second visit to earth and was inhabiting the body of the earthly female Ti (HG "Do's Intro: What Our Purpose Is—The Simple 'Bottom Line,'" 1–2).[9]

According to HG beliefs,[10] we perpetually reincarnate as human beings without change or progress; however, humans can metamorphose to the Next Level if stimulated by multiple interactions with Next Level beings. During their previous visit, Ti and Do had initiated the transfiguration process through teachings and classes with a number of promising students. Learning that earth was about to expire, they returned to locate and graduate the reincarnations of promising students before the demise of the planet. The window of time allotted to the task was short. The appearance of the Hale-Bopp comet was, for Do, a sign of the end. The group modified its homepage. The words "Red Alert" flashed at the top, and white-letter text explained that Hale-Bopp was the final marker.[11]

According to Web-published autobiographical writings,[12] Do was unsure whether the group was supposed to respond to the marker by "laying down" the human bodies they occupied, at which point they would be assumed into TELAH bodies. His hope was that they would be taken directly to the Next Level aboard a spaceship whose presence Do

believed was masked by the comet tail. Pondering which course to take, Do wrote, "If my Father does not require this disposition of us, He will take us up into His cloud of light before such laying down of bodies need occur." When the cloud of light did not arrive, Do evidently concluded that a bodily laying down was necessary. His followers accepted Do's conclusion, with mass death the result.

It is important to realize that HG members did not casually abandon the bodies they had ceased to value. Quite the contrary: they used them to form a last evangelical message. Through extraordinary effort, they arranged their soon-to-be-discarded vehicles into a striking image that testified to the ritual intentionality behind their deaths. The one surprising contradiction to HG's blatantly public end was that the group failed to Webcast the death process. It was as though, at the very end, members opted merely to leave the bizarre death mask their bodies formed for whoever found it.

An online virtual epitaph coined by one HG member consisted of a poignant plea to the world to understand what the group was about to do:

Now, all this talk of the Second Coming? Guess what? It's really here! We are at the End of the Age, where it is our understanding that all minds/souls are back for another chance to choose what path they wish to pursue. And what I know from my Teachers is that the time has come for this Next Level classroom to close, and for us to make the transition from this world to Our Father's World. What I also know, in my heart, is that my Older Members [Ti and Do] bear the only truth there is. They are what we've all been waiting for, and for anyone to doubt their worth is literally playing with fire, and, to use my Older Members' words, "that's the Gospel!" Personally, I simply cannot imagine anyone not jumping for JOY and lapping this information up, but then I am actually living this truth, so my perspective, as well as my expectations, are more real and exciting. It's much like Jonah and the Whale, for one has to actually do this to know it

HG "EXIT STATEMENT"

In spite of the cyberspace effort of Heaven's Gate to justify its members' deaths, the public responded with horror, shock, and ridicule but little empathy. Media portrayals painted HG adherents as peculiar, odd, and radically different from the rest of us. HG jokes abounded, a sign of widespread, public irresolution over exactly what had occurred and why. *Did you hear about the new paint job on Dr. Kevorkian's van? It's a Nike swoosh with the words "Just Do It" stenciled underneath.*

As the boundaries between religion and other cultural creeds thin, the ability of traditional religions to adjudicate interpretation of their myths and symbols is diminished. A traditional religious apocalypticist who announces a plan to rebuild the temple in Jerusalem or a date for the return of Jesus is immediately confronted by priests, rabbis, and established interpreters of the tradition who demand proof and justification. These demands create an apocalyptic firebreak that can slow, if not halt, the spread of the enthusiasm. If the authorized interpreters of a religion declare that the ideas associated with an apocalyptic outbreak are outside the range of accepted doctrine, this can further reduce its appeal.

Absent these mechanisms of interpretive restraint, the Heaven's Gate beliefs were almost completely devoid of firebreak potential. It proved a deadly deficiency, while the group's participation in cyberspace provided just enough of a global audience to give HG members fatal assurance that their departure would not go unnoticed. In this, at least, they were right.

Mary in Cyberspace: The Divine Female as Prophetess

Christianity came to life as an expressly apocalyptic new religious movement. Mary, the mother of Jesus, founder of the movement, was consigned a small role in the Christian biblical texts that purport to account for this beginning. Only in the gospel of Luke did she attain a lyrical position as the divinely chosen vehicle of Jesus' birth. Little in the meager historical record that informs our understanding of the first centuries of Christian tradition suggests that Mary was of more than minor significance during the origins of the movement. Yet from the third century on, Mary was transformed into a major force in Roman Catholic tradition.[13] The grassroots Christian faithful came to declare Mary herself an apocalypse—a revelation from God.

The apocalyptic belief that Jesus would soon return and transform the earth was cherished by first-century Christians, but starting with Augustine in the fourth century, Christian authorities turned away from these chiliastic tendencies, and they were soon declared heresy by church leaders. The church alone was to be the vehicle of God on Earth. Forced underground, the Christian apocalyptic tradition did not disappear. Instead, it became linked to the popular religious Cult of Mary and has remained an aspect of Marian veneration ever since.[14] Whenever end-of-time fears erupt in Catholic tradition, they tend to do so first in the subcurrent of Marian devotion.

Since then, Marian devotionalism has flourished among the laity, but scant authoritative support for Marian veneration has emerged. A consensus among historians of the tradition indicates that the elevation of Mary's official stature, through adoption of doctrines such as her immaculate conception and bodily assumption into heaven, is significantly attributable to the capitulation of reluctant church authorities to grassroots pressures.[15]

After the sixteenth century Protestant schism, Marianism virtually vanished as a resource of religious piety among those allied with the newly born Protestant wing of Christian tradition. In part, this aided Protestant efforts to distinguish themselves from their powerful parent in the Latin West. Yet in the Roman Catholic tradition, as well as in the Eastern Orthodox churches, the cult of Mary remained a hugely generative component of religious life. Practically all acts of personal devotion widely practiced by Catholics and Eastern Orthodox today had their genesis in Marian veneration.[16]

In the theological aftermath of two world wars fought largely among Christian nations, traditional Christologies became destabilized. Rushing to fill the void was Marian veneration. For the Catholic faithful, whenever historical context made the reality of an omnipotent God difficult to grasp, the tender comfort of Mary proved irresistible. Then came cyberspace, which introduced a fresh differential into the centuries-old tension between popular Marian devotionalism and official Marian resistance. Previously a fount of innovative pietism that nourished Christian tradition more or less behind the scenes, the Cult of Mary was now on global display.

This newfound publicity pumped energy into an already resurgent Marian devotionalism. At the turn of the millennium, the Cult of Mary is at an all-time high. Only the twelfth century rivals the twentieth for Marian sitings, and the demographics of modernity ensure than not even the massive medieval Cult of Mary in the Latin West could numerically rival the popularity Mary evokes in the modern world. From the Blue Army of Fatima supporters to the Marian movement of priests (with which, incidentally, a key leader of the RTCG was closely associated during his formative years of priestly training), Marian groups are a mighty force in contemporary Christian tradition.

An influential repository of Marian apocalypticism in cyberspace is the Virgin Mary in America site. As sedate, funereal organ music plays in the background, the site opens with a bold claim:

Give Me That Online Religion

The Apocalypse is now! Armageddon—the great Battle for souls—is raging! The physical Battle in Palestine lies just ahead! The Reign of Antichrist began in 1971! The prophecies of the end times are presently unfolding! Read and learn about the apparitions, revelations, messages, prophecies, visions, miracles given through the visionary Veronica Lueken.

HTTP://WWW.HURSTLINKS.COM/VIRGINMARY/INDEX.HTML

The major link the site promotes is the Bayside Story Website, which tells the story of Veronica Lueken. That site's welcome page (www.roses.org/ intro/welcome.htm) opens with gold script letters announcing "The Bayside Story" on a white background. A head-and-shoulders photograph of Veronica when she was a chubby-faced Bayside, Queens, New York, housewife hovers in the lower left-hand corner. Veronica's curly black hair is almost totally hidden by a lacy white veil. She clutches a crucifix in one hand, and her face is in a position such that she appears to be gazing up at the letters over the photo that identify the site.

The site gives a brief summary of Lueken's background as a Marian mystic. She lived from 1923 to 1995 and became widely known in the last two decades of her life as "the seer of Bayside."

A married woman, and a mother of five children. Up until June of 1968, she lived the life of an ordinary New York City housewife, with her husband Arthur, a retired purchasing agent, and their daughter and four sons. On the day that Robert F. Kennedy was shot to death in California by an assassin, Veronica experienced a perfume of roses when she responded to a radio appeal for prayers for the dying Senator. A short time later, St. Teresa the Little Flower . . . appeared to her. Her early visions seemed to be a sort of preparation for the coming of Our Lady, who announced to her in 1970 that She wanted Rosary Vigils held outdoors on the eves of all the great feast days of the Catholic Church. . . . She promised if these Vigils would be faithfully kept, despite weather conditions and disturbances, She would appear to Veronica at each of the Vigils, and give heavenly messages of worldwide importance.

HTTP://WWW.HURSTLINKS.COM/VIRGINMARY/STORY.HTML

Thousands were convinced that Veronica Lueken's visions were authentic. Until 1975, public vigils were kept in Bayside Hills in accordance with the strictures of Lueken's visions. In 1975, crowd pressures led to relocation of the vigils from Bayside to the Vatican Pavilion at the old World's Fair grounds in Flushing Meadows, New York.

According to the background of the Bayside Story, the messages Lueken received from Mary were fiercely apocalyptic:

> The Messages reveal the general state of evil in the world, the state of corruption within the Catholic Church, the evil within the Vatican itself, and the necessity of worldwide atonement to the Eternal Father to avoid chastisements, which, if not mitigated by universal penance and return to God and His Divine Laws, will be terrible beyond comprehension. They warn that a worldwide Warning, Miracle, and fiery Chastisement in the form of a "Ball of Redemption"—a comet which will strike the earth, and along with World War III and other disasters that will remove three-quarters of mankind are near at hand.

HTTP://WWW.HURSTLINKS.COM/VIRGINMARY/STORY.HTML

The site authors go to great length to defend their report of Marian visions as a legitimate Roman Catholic practice. They explain that even though some bishops have attempted to ban dissemination of Lueken's visions, this represents an overstepping of their legitimate authority. The site authors contend that as of 1967, canon 1939, which forbade publishing books "such as those that deal with revelations, visions, prophecies and miracles," was overturned.[17] In boldfaced and underlined text, they conclude their justification argument with the assertion that publishing Lueken's prophecies is within the bounds of acceptable Catholic practice:

> This means that henceforth: Catholics are permitted without need of Imprimatur, or of Nihil Obstat, or any other permission, to publish accounts of revelations, visions, prophecies and miracles. Of course these publications must not put in danger the Faith or the Morals: this is the general rule which every Catholic must follow in all his actions. . . .

HTTP://WWW.HURSTLINKS.COM/VIRGINMARY/CHURCH.HTML

Sociologist Michael Cuneo has extensively studied the Bayside group. He refers to the apocalyptic Mary of Veronica Lueken and her followers as the "vengeful virgin."[18] Yet the "miraculous photo" included in the Lueken Website, putatively taken of Mary in December 1999, fails to depict a vengeful figure. The fuzzy image in white—to the extent it resembles anything at all—looks more like Tinkerbell than Kali.

Because many who claim to have experienced Marian sitings insist that Mary uttered prophetic messages about the end of time, church organizations encourage Marian devotees to interpret her messages as a peace-producing apocalyptic. The FAQ on Marian sightings published by the Marian Library and International Marian Research Institute at the University of Dayton, Ohio, a historically Marianist school, furnishes an excellent example of the Catholic church's ongoing effort to defuse a potentially schismatic Marian apocalypticism.

The reports and stories of Our Lady's re-appearances on earth serve to remind the Church that she has a special mission to help Christians amidst the routine of their daily life in this modern world. Mary is Our Lady of the End Times. She is a caring instrument of the Holy Spirit who constantly intercedes for us before God. By her life, her activities in heaven, and the many reports of her re-appearances today, Mary has given the Church a message of hope and redemption. The key to receiving Mary's message is our disposition and attitude. May we strive to make this time an Age of Mary through devotion to her and by instilling in our lives a passionate dedication of service to God and our fellow man.

HTTP://WWW.UDAYTON.EDU/MARY

As Marian groups become increasingly involved with cyberspace, the thick apocalypticism affiliated with Marianist practices has become less constrained to Marianist circles and more publicly visible; consequently, the cult's potential to infuse Christian tradition with apocalyptic fervor is increasingly obvious. Though admittedly at the level of pure speculation, a desire to head off a wave of Marian-inspired apocalypticism during the year 2000 may have strengthened Pope John Paul II's commitment to proclaim 2000 the Year of Jubilee and encourage devotional pilgrimages to Rome, Jerusalem, Nazareth, and Bethlehem. Better to have a controlled, intrachurch apocalyptic enthusiasm acted out on the church's main stage than have unregulated apocalyptic enthusiasm erupt in the shadows of the tradition.

Marketing the End: The Van Prophecy Portal

Evangelical Christians make up roughly one-fifth of the U.S. population. United by commonly held end-times beliefs, evangelicals cherish the apocalyptic. Going far beyond the technical meaning scholars intend when they bring the term *apocalyptic* into play, evangelical Christians treat the entire Christian bible as an apocalypse or revelation.

According to mainstream evangelical thinking, eternal salvation for all human beings is the fruit of having a "living relationship with God." But starting this relationship requires public confession to key evangelical beliefs, most crucially that Jesus is Lord. To evangelicals, everyone outside the charmed circle of beliefs they inhabit flounders and sinks in the ocean of time. Those within it live. At the end of time, any opportunity others have to adopt evangelical beliefs disappears. The end, they believe, could come at any moment.

Consequently, there is an intrinsic urgency to evangelicals' beliefs that obliges them to communicate what they believe quickly and widely to others. Christian evangelicals were among the first to promote their religious beliefs on radio, then on television, and then in cyberspace. They began launching Websites before 90 percent of Americans knew what a Website was.

Fundamentalists are a subset of evangelical Christians. They hold the same beliefs as evangelicals, but the bulk of believers on either side of the theological fence separating them would claim that fundamentalists hold those beliefs more fiercely. One area where the difference is quite evident is willingness to cooperate with others. Evangelicals work with nonevangelicals to accomplish a common goal. Fundamentalists cooperate only with other fundamentalists.

Taking a tough stand on their beliefs, fundamentalists left more moderate Christian institutions in the early twentieth century to build a separatist fundamentalist subculture. Filling and funding the institutions and congregations that were the basis of the subculture required recruits. To survive, fundamentalists aggressively exploited new media to advocate their beliefs and persuade others to join them—sometimes even more avidly than their evangelical kin. In cyberspace, fundamentalists were Christianity's initial pioneers.

Online, fundamentalist groups distinguish themselves from other Christian streams by a propensity to treat the apocalyptic as a starting point for faith.

Online, fundamentalist groups distinguish themselves from other Christian streams by a propensity to treat the apocalyptic as a starting point for faith. The Websites of the ministry of Jack Van Impe demonstrate this tendency well. But Van Impe did not begin his ministry in cyberspace. He started as a mainstream, fundamentalist evangelist and then in the early 1980s took up electronic preaching, starting with television. Though he failed to garner the national prominence of Jerry Falwell, Oral Roberts, or Pat Robertson, Van Impe became a stalwart member of the Christian fundamentalist televangelism wave.

He continues the involvement to this day by means of a weekly television show, *Jack Van Impe Presents*. Like most fundamentalist preachers who chose the electronic church, Van Impe did not stick with this one medium but quickly diversified his ministries into a multimedia format.

Today the Van Impe fundamentalist empire includes international television, radio, video, film, and print media ministries.

Van Impe's launch into cyberspace came in 1995, when another ministry invited him to take over a preexisting Website, according to an e-mail sent by the current Van Impe Webmaster:

Another ministry had space left on [its] host server and had offered to help us get a website online for free. It started as just a little something extra we would have available.

Signaling a fundamentalist commitment to biblical literalism and emphasis on end-times belief, Van Impe named his Website the Prophecy Portal (www.jvim.com) and stocked it with arguments, interspersed with biblical quotes, as to why the Christian Bible should be read as a repository of predictions about the future.

Van Impe's involvement in cyberspace, begun as a side venture, deepened over time. When it became clear to the ministry that the site's popularity was expanding, additional personnel and computer resources were tapped to keep it going. After five years, the Van Impe site has traveled far from its humble secondhand beginnings. Today it employs three servers, is monitored by a full-time Web programmer, and receives regular volunteer support from a Web design and development company.

The heavy investment of resources Van Impe has made into the ministry's Website is apparent. The Prophecy Portal is slickly designed, with frequent use of Java and other interactive macros to delight the eye and prolong interest in the site. It also offers myriad links, to such sites as the Trinity Broadcasting Network, National Religious Broadcasters, the Bible Gateway, and the God Channel.

Physically, the main welcome page that anchors the Van Impe site combines the banal with the bizarre. Representing the banal, the main page sports a white background with a thin blue banner at the top. In sedate white letters, the banner welcomes visitors to Jack Van Impe

Ministries International. Underneath the welcome banner is a drawing of the earth. A dove etched in red and yellow flame hovers over it.

Introducing the bizarre, an inch-wide swath of red and black cuts through the middle of the site. Superimposed over this second banner in large gold print are the words "Apocalypse II: The Revelation. The Book has been opened." Immediately to the right of these words, a sinister-looking pair of dark eyes with simmering red pupils glare at anyone who dares to read the page. Clicking on the banner leads to an image: the front of the video box containing the Van Impe ministries' latest end-times film. It can be ordered, one learns, for $29.95, exclusively from Van Impe and is also available on DVD.

To Van Impe, the biblical book of Revelation is particularly exciting because it gives people the tools necessary to decipher human history as the plan of God:

The Book of Revelation, the last book of the Bible, is the point at which all the prophecies of the ages converge and find their ultimate fulfillment. Within its pages are specific details concerning the return of the Lord Jesus Christ to earth, the establishment of His Millenial [*sic*] kingdom, and finally, the eternal state of both the saved and the lost.

Farther down in this same section of the site, in an area titled "Bible Prophecy and You," Van Impe explains why the end of time is near:

Current international events reflect exactly the conditions and happenings predicted throughout the Bible for the last days of this age. Remember that this special message has been given to reveal God's truth, not conceal it; and to clarify God's eternal purpose, not mystify it. Millions need to be alerted to the fact that Jesus is coming soon-perhaps today! We all need to be ready and "Looking for that Blessed Hope, and the glorious appearing of the great God and our Saviour Jesus Christ" (Titus 2:13).

HTTP://WWW.JVIM.COM/MESSAGES/BPANDY.HTML

Van Impe's Prophecy Portal claims that horrible times are ahead for humanity. In a section titled "Intelligence Briefing, Signs of the End Times and Christ's Return," Van Impe writes:

It is a spectacular, never-before-seen, earth-shattering event whose merciful objective is to prove to earth dwellers that the One who comes from heaven is indeed the Son of God, the One who is to be received with joy and thanksgiving. . . . But will the inhabitants of earth be joyful? Hardly. Revelation 1:7 tells us, *Behold, he cometh with clouds; and every eye shall see him, and they also which pierced him: and all kindreds of the earth shall wail because of him.* So, they will not rejoice? With meteors showering their land, and darkness settling on the earth, and heavenly armies rising up to do battle against evil, one could safely assume that few earth dwellers will be saying to their neighbors, *have a nice day.* It will not seem like a pleasant day at all. We are told that the earth dwellers will mourn.

HTTP://WWW.JVIM.COM/INTELLIGENCEBRIEFING/JANUARY2000/COVER.HTML

According to the Van Impe Webmaster, heavy complimentary feedback from those who access the site is customary.

We have received overwhelmingly positive feedback from our website globally. . . . Since we started tracking response, we have had over 6 million visits (not hits) to our website. We now average between [9,000 and] 10,000 visits per day.

The Van Impe site offers a treasure trove of popular apocalyptic materials. One can order dozens of short films on the apocalyptic, with such titles as *Antichrist: Super Deceiver of the New World Order, Apocalypse Code,* and *Armageddon—The Beginning or the End.* None is over ninety minutes long, and some are as short as fifteen minutes.

There are Bibles available with special apocalyptic notes. For those who order them soon, Van Impe promises to include his "Overview of Major Future Events." It consists of a one-page color drawing. At the top left, a world in swirling white represents creation. Underneath it, three empty wooden crosses are drawn in red and orange. Mounted on a hillside, they represent the crucifixion of Christ and the two thieves. To their immediate right, a raging battle on horseback is shown. It depicts the final conflict at Armageddon.

Underneath the visual depiction of the earth's history, Van Impe provides a skeletal outline of the past, present, and future of the world as he understands it. The major headings Van Impe employs to diagram what he contends is earth's immediate future are the "Battle of Armageddon," the "Judgment of the Nations," the "1,000-Year Reign of Christ," "Satan Loosed/The Final Rebellion," and "Resurrection of the Unsaved for Great White Throne Judgment." The Van Impe history of the earth concludes with the somewhat disturbing "Purification and Renewal of the Earth and Heavens." The entire document takes about five minutes to read. Consisting of one page, it can be readily mounted on a home or office wall for easy reference. Truly, this is the history of the world made simple!

Not all materials offered on the Van Impe site have a price tag; the Prophecy Portal is stocked with a few freebies as well. They include an end-times bumper sticker, a subscription to the "Prophecy Portal" newsletter, and several online apocalyptic books. The free weekly prophecy e-mailing started in November 1999 has proved especially popular. Van Impe ministries boast that they e-mail their prophecy newsletter to more than thirty thousand people each week.

Overall, fundamentalists like Van Impe figuratively and literally market the end. They do so figuratively through a prodigious and amazingly successful endeavor to popularize end-times beliefs. After all, until the nineteenth century, the apocalyptic was a pursuit of cultural elites. Now apocalypticism thrives in the realm of popular culture in part because preachers such as Van Impe have demonstrated tremendous effectiveness in popularizing it. Van Impe markets the end literally by offering for sale a huge number of products related to end times. The cumulative effect of the Van Impe site, coupled with other apocalyptic popularizing ventures such as the Bible Code and the Left Behind series, is that a heavy scent of apocalypticism saturates contemporary Christianity. Constrained neither to fundamentalist circles nor the wider evangelical subculture, apocalypticism permeates Christianity's many manifestations.

Yale theologian George Lindbeck assigns responsibility for the strongly apocalyptic, messianic character of contemporary Christianity to the collapse of what he calls "Christologies from above." Lindbeck contends that as the bloody twentieth century chipped away at the believability of a cosmic, omnipotent Christ, Christian belief in Christ's immanence became more difficult to sustain. Catholics responded with increasing appreciation for Mary. But the sixteenth-century Christian schism foreclosed this avenue for Protestants; among them, a desire for Christ to come again as Messiah swelled. The Van Impe Prophecy Portal is one of a huge number of Christian fundamentalist places where this interest is elicited and apocalyptic desire is cultivated, strengthened, and augmented.

The Risks and Rewards of the Virtual End

For good or ill, CMC significantly increases the potential for apocalyptic ideas to spread through and across human societies. These communications also make it easier for apocalyptic groups to become household names. Formerly characterized by a certain social and ideological distance from society at large, apocalyptic groups with few resources can now promote themselves via the Internet to an international audience, enlist others to their worldview, and coordinate the actions of adherents across geopolitical borders. Most now do so.

Infrequently, apocalyptic individuals and groups turn violent. Because the Internet is a prevailing means of organization and communication for apocalypticists, the struggle between groups aflame with apocalyptic enthusiasm and having a propensity for violence, on the one hand, and those whose goal is preserving civil order, on the other, takes place in multiple sites. They are electronic as well as geographical, virtual as well as actual, and concerned with geographically dispersed as well as geographically concentrated congregations.

Because it openly addresses the potential tie between apocalypticism and religious violence, this brief tour of the virtual apocalyptic risks defining end-times belief as a harmful social force; however, such a completely negative assessment of the apocalyptic is not warranted. Even though end-times enthusiasm can compel people to disrupt the status quo, apocalyptic disruptions are not inevitably detrimental to human well-being. Contra Marx, apocalypticism can furnish a divine ground for self-respect among the oppressed. For people ensnared in profoundly unjust social systems, belief in divine judgment can be a source of life-giving energy when human judgment appears to have become completely perverted. As a seed of hope it is small, but one that possesses the potential to fuel liberatory social action.

Apocalypticism in cyberspace is a social force that must be handled with care. Like the atom, dreams of world judgment contain tremendous energy.

Given this, apocalypticism in cyberspace is a social force that must be handled with care. Like the atom, dreams of world judgment contain tremendous energy. When tapped, they can inspire revolts, promote economic or social justice, or convince thirty-nine people to kill themselves. One of the central challenges we face as citizens of numerous nations is to build societies in which people's *yetser tov*, or inclination toward good, can flourish while their *yetser hara*, or inclination toward evil, is restrained. Because the Internet facilitates distributing apocalyptic messages, it could contribute to an increase in the number and size of apocalyptic groups if the individuals exposed to virtual apocalyptic missives prove a receptive audience. Developing healthy civil societies for the third millennium requires that the dangers of cyberspace-enhanced apocalyptic fever be contained while its capacity to motivate us to believe in and therefore create just societies be allowed to flourish.

Seeing a Flame There: Religion and the Future of Cyberspace

In each generation, a segment of humanity searches for a personal encounter with the ground of life's meaning. These spiritual explorers have bequeathed records of their experiences to subsequent generations in a variety of forms. Religious sculpture, painting, music, codes of behavior, ritual, texts, and whole organizations that populate the present testify to their accomplishments.

One great contribution of contemporary scholarship has been theory and analysis that improve our critical thinking about this inheritance. A hallmark of the work of scholars such as Elisabeth Schüssler-Fiorenza and Ellen M. Umansky is careful, precise investigation of the extent to which the act of carrying forward religious tradition has been neither naïve nor innocent of political dimensions.[1] Instead, it has been selective, with the voices and experiences of certain groups steadfastly omitted.

Given the cracks in our spiritual heritage that historical, archaeological, and sociological studies have revealed, the present generation faces an immense challenge as it undertakes establishing its own relationship with the transcendent. Finding a meaningful God in the present is difficult when one must question, rather than rely on, insights from the past. But there is no way around that task if this generation is to have a healthy spiritual dimension. Ultimately, only individuals who encounter the divine as a vibrant aspect of their life and world and relate to it as a living reality keep humanity's religious endeavor going.

For the sacred to have substance, each generation must articulate ideas of the divine that are credible and meaningful against the backdrop of its time. Skipping or mishandling this task can cause an eclipse of the divine. Encounters with the sacred as told by past generations took place in their daily lives. Moses saw a burning bush on the mountain near where he tended sheep. The angel Gabriel came to Mohammed in the desert through which passed the caravans on which he worked. Jesus taught in the plains, hills, and cities where people gathered. Each was responded to by people in his day as an in-breaking of the transcendent that made the divine believable.

Cyberspace is a dominant component of the landscape of the twenty-first century. The pioneers of online religion described in this book are finding a viable sign of the transcendent within its domain. There is an odd similarity between what religious people expect of their relationship with the divine and what computer users expect of cyberspace. Websites crash if an extraordinary number of people attempt to log on to them at once, but ordinarily, perfect, multiple accessibility is a cardinal quality of cyberspace. People are disappointed and angry if they cannot access the Website they seek. It seems wrong, a contradiction of the universe, for a Website not to be available, because the Web, like Krishna and Mary, is supposed to be always available, always listening, and always responsive, no matter how many people are dancing around. Whether the wanderers through the mountains, deserts, and hills of cyberspace will persuasively articulate their online encounter with the divine remains to be seen. But like Moses, these people have climbed up a virtual mountain because they saw a flame there.

My hope is that we can marshal the public will necessary to preserve cyberspace as a place where they may continue to climb and roam. To induce people to undertake this stance, I offer reasons ranging from the social to the existential and the mystical.

Socially, in spite of its pitfalls and dangers, religion in cyberspace offers a valuable countervailing presence to the market commodification of everything in sight. Governments cannot provide this. Religion can.

Existentially, the aspiration for intelligible expression of the transcendent motivates billions. Corporations cannot satisfy this longing, but religion can because it specializes in limited, finite, human attempts to make sense of these encounters.

Mystically, humanity's search for a direct encounter with the divine has been fulfilled by the widely accepted stories of the encounters of a rare few in human history. Would we cut off cyberspace as a place where this might occur? In mythic terms, this is an act akin to leveling the mountain before Moses can see on it a fire that does not consume itself.

We have a wonderful opportunity to exercise maximum influence on how cyberspace develops, but that opportunity diminishes as our habits of interaction with cyberspace become set.

We have a wonderful opportunity to exercise maximum influence on how cyberspace develops, but that opportunity diminishes as our habits of interaction with cyberspace become set. Taking the historical and critical lessons of contemporary scholarship to heart, we need to be aware that the shape of religion and spirituality in the future are likely to be determined by the individuals who participate in virtual religion now. If we opt to maintain cyberspace as a public domain where religious expression can freely occur, it will be but a first step, given the complexity of contemporary religion. The formidable tasks that will immediately confront us include determining how we can support religion in cyberspace while preserving its diversity and how we can support religion in cyberspace while avoiding the leveling effect of hegemonic globalization. The challenges of accepting cyberspace as a public common where religious expression is welcome are immense, but the rewards may be equally vast.

Notes

Chapter 1. A Revolution in the Making: Spiritual Wonder Goes Online

1. A. N. Whitehead, *Religion in the Making: Lowell Lectures, 1926* (Old Tappan, N.J.: Macmillan, 1926).

2. Private conversation with Rabbi Lawrence Zierler, Jan. 2000.

3. D. S. Landes, *Revolution in Time: Clocks and the Making of the Modern World* (Cambridge, Mass.: Belknap Press, 1983).

4. M. U. Edwards Jr., *Printing, Propaganda, and Martin Luther* (Berkeley: University of California Press, 1994).

5. S. Freud, *The Future of an Illusion,* trans. J. Strachey (New York: Norton, 1989; originally published 1927).

6. F. Nietzsche, *The Gay Science* (New York: Random House, 1974; originally published 1887), p. 181.

7. A. N. Whitehead, *Process and Reality* (New York: Free Press, 1979).

8. W. C. Smith, *Toward a World Theology: Faith and the Comparative History of Religion* (Louisville, Ky.: Westminster/John Knox, 1981).

9. H. Smith, *The World's Religions* (San Francisco: HarperSanFrancisco, 1991).

10. W. S. Bainbridge and R. Stark, *A Theory of Religion* (New Brunswick, N.J.: Rutgers University Press, 1996).

Chapter 2. The Ultimate Diaspora: Religion in the Perpetual Present of Cyberspace

1. E. J. Gorn, "Professing History: Distinguishing Between Memory and the Past," *Chronicle of Higher Education,* 2000, *46,* B4–B5.

2. W. Gibson, *Neuromancer* (New York: Ace Science Fiction Books, 1984).

3. W. G. Robinson, "Heaven's Gate: The End?" *Journal of Computer Mediated Communication,* 1997, *3*(3). Online publication: <http://www.ascusc.org/jcmc/vol3/issue3/robinson.html>.

4. D. F. Noble, *The Religion of Technology: The Divinity of Man and the Spirit of Invention* (New York: Knopf, 1997); F. Ferre, *Hellfire and Lightning Rods: Liberating Science, Technology, and Religion* (Maryknoll, N.Y.: Orbis Books, 1993).

5. M. U. Edwards Jr., *Printing, Propaganda, and Martin Luther* (Berkeley: University of California Press, 1994).

6. J. Cobb, *Cybergrace: The Search for God in Cyberspace* (New York: Crown Books, 1998).

Chapter 3. A Taste of Forever: Cyberspace as Sacred Time

1. W. M. Pfeiffer, *Cyberspace and Time* <http://www.monarchbreeze.com/views6_cyberspace_and_time.html>. Accessed Jan. 2000.

2. Ibid.

3. Ibid.

4. "Mark of the beast 666" is a reference to a belief popular among Christian fundamentalists that an evil entity marked with the number 666 would appear at the end of time.

5. The 700 Club <http://www.cbn.org/the700club/>. Accessed May 3, 1999.

Chapter 5. Cyber-Virtue and Cyber-Vice

1. The Jenni-Cam site allows visitors sufficient access to judge whether they want to get involved with the site. You can check it out at <http://www.jennicam.org/j2kr/index.html>.

2. M. A. Smith and P. Kollock, *Communities in Cyberspace* (New York: Routledge, 1999).

3. A. Kemp and B. Wazir, "The Cyber Warriors: Inside the Hacker's Web," *Observer,* Feb. 13, 2000, p. 19.

4. H. Rheingold, *The Virtual Community: Homesteading on the Electronic Frontier* (Reading, Mass.: Addison-Wesley, 1993).

5. Ibid.

6. The femrel-l homepage is <http://www.io.com/~jenab/femrel/>. Archives of recent femrel-l messages can be found at <http://listserv.aol.com/archives/femrel-l.html>.

7. W. S. Bainbridge and R. Stark, *A Theory of Religion* (New Brunswick, N.J.: Rutgers University Press, 1996).

8. Private e-mail correspondence, May 1999.

9. J. Cobb, *Cybergrace: The Search for God in Cyberspace* (New York: Crown Books, 1998).

Chapter 6. Virtual Shrines and the Cult of Celebrity

1. H. Rheingold, *The Virtual Community: Homesteading on the Electronic Frontier* (Reading, Mass.: Addison-Wesley, 1993).

2. C. Summer, "Hollywood Tangled Up in Web," Dec. 11, 1996 <http://www.teleport.com/~btucker/bbuhpnuz.txt>. Accessed Jan. 28, 2000.

Chapter 7. Existential Doubt, or Does a Cyborg Have a Soul?

1. P. L. Berger and T. Luckmann, *The Social Construction of Reality: A Treatise in the Sociology of Knowledge* (New York: Doubleday, 1967).

2. R. Williams, *Television, Technology, and Cultural Form* (New York: Schocken Books, 1974), p. 13.

3. S. Zuboff, *In the Age of the Smart Machine: The Future of Work and Power* (New York: Basic Books, 1988).

4. N. Stephenson, *Snow Crash* (New York: Bantam Books, 1993).

5. M. E. Clynes and N. S. Kline, "Cyborgs and Space," in C. H. Gray (ed.), *The Cyborg Handbook* (New York: Routledge, 1995).

6. R. Barthes, *Mythologies,* trans. A. Lavers (New York: Hill & Wang, 1972).

7. D. J. Haraway, "Manifesto for Cyborgs: Science, Technology and Socialist-Feminist Perspective in the 1980s," *Socialist Review,* 1985, *80,* 65–108.

8. Ibid., p. 81.

9. N. Goldenberg, *Resurrecting the Body: Feminism, Religion, and Psycho Analysis* (New York: Crossroad, 1993; originally published as *Returning Words to Flesh,* 1990).

10. Ibid., p. 17.

11. Ibid., p. 11.

12. I. Barbour, *Ethics in an Age of Technology: The Gifford Lectures 2* (San Francisco: HarperSanFrancisco, 1993), p. 24.

13. Ibid., p. 26.

14. G. Goethals, *The Electronic Golden Calf: Images, Religion, and the Making of Meaning* (Cambridge, Mass.: Dowley, 1990), p. 188.

15. Ibid., p. 189.

16. J.-P. Baudrillard, *Cool Memories,* trans. C. Turner (London: Verso, 1987).

17. H. Ruppersberg, "The Alien Messiah," in A. Kuhn (ed.), *Alien Zone: Cultural Theory and Contemporary Science Fiction Cinema* (London: Verso, 1990).

18. J. Radway, *Reading the Romance: Feminism and the Representation of Women in Popular Culture* (Chapel Hill: University of North Carolina Press, 1984).

19. P. Brooks, *The Melodramatic Imagination: Balzac, Henry James, Melodrama, and the Mode of Excess* (New Haven, Conn.: Yale University Press, 1976).

20. D. J. Haraway, *Simians, Cyborgs, and Women: The Re-Invention of Nature* (New York: Routledge, 1991).

Chapter 8. Virtual Prophets, Instant Global Access, and the Apocalypse

1. G. Gorenberg, *The End of Days: Fundamentalism and the Struggle for the Temple Mount* (New York: Free Press, 2000).

2. A. Haselkorn, "Japan's Poison Gas Apocalyptics," *American Spectator*, July 28, 1995, pp. 22–25.

3. M. Introvigne, "Tragedy in Uganda: The Restoration of the Ten Commandments of God, a Post-Catholic Movement," Apr. 5, 2000 <http://www.cesnur.org/testi/uganda_002.htm>. Accessed Apr. 26, 2000.

4. Personal conversation with Richard Landes at the Millennium 2000 conference, Neve Ilan, Israel, May 1999.

5. Personal conversation with Gershom Gorenberg in Jerusalem, Dec. 1998.

6. W. G. Robinson, "Heaven's Gate: The End?" *Journal of Computer Mediated Communication*, 1997, *3*(3). Online publication: <http://www.ascusc.org/jcmc/vol3/issue3/robinson.html>. Accessed Nov. 11, 1998.

7. Heaven's Gate, "Heaven's Gate: How and When It May Be Entered" <http://www.zdnet.com/yil/higher/heavensgate/index.html>. Accessed June 1998.

8. Ibid.

9. Ibid.

10. Ibid.

11. Ibid.

12. Ibid.

13. M. Hamington, *Hail Mary? The Struggle for Ultimate Womanhood in Catholicism* (New York: Routledge, 1995).

14. M. W. Cuneo, "The Vengeful Virgin: Case Studies in Contemporary American Catholic Apocalypticism," in T. Robbins and S. J. Palmer (eds.), *Millennium, Messiahs, and Mayhem* (New York: Routledge, 1997).

15. Hamington, *Hail Mary?*

16. Ibid.

17. Background information on Roman Cathlic canon law can be found at the New Advent Website <http://www.newadvent.org/cathen/09056a.htm>, under "Canon Law." Detailed information on canon law is also available via the Vatican Website <http://www.vatican.va>.

18. Cuneo, "Vengeful Virgin."

Epilogue

1. E. Schüssler Fiorenza, *In Memory of Her: A Feminist Theological Reconstruction of Christian Origins* (New York: Crossroad, 1983); E. M. Umansky, "Teaching Jewish Studies," in M. Peskowitz and L. Levitt (eds.), *Judaism Since Gender* (New York: Routledge, 1997).

The Author

As at home on the Internet as in a classroom or researching real-life religious communities, Brenda Brasher has tracked online religion for more than a decade. Intrigued by comparative religion as a young child, she opted to turn her avocation into a vocation by earning a master's degree in divinity from Christian Theological Seminary and a Ph.D. in religion from the University of Southern California. Now an assistant professor of religion and philosophy at Mount Union College in Alliance, Ohio, she spends part of each year in the Middle East studying its poignant nexus of international religious piety and conflict.

A lover of horses, cats, small dogs, and Hong Kong cinema, she is an avid traveler and poet. A much-published author, her first book—*Godly Women: Fundamentalism and Female Power*—was named an Outstanding Academic Book of 1998 by Choice.

Index

image in, 20; impact on future of religion, 19–23; linkages and convergence in, 29–30; pioneers, 69–70; political argument for, 6–7; reconfiguration of, 42–43. *See also* Popular-culture religions

Oral cultures, memory in, 37–38

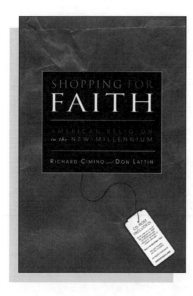

Shopping for Faith

*American Religion in
the New Millennium*

Richard Cimino and Don Lattin

$25.00 Hardcover,
CD-ROM included
ISBN 0-7879-4170-0

"Shopping for Faith is as good as it gets in assessing the U.S. religion scene at millennium's end. Cimino and Lattin present a picture of multiple trends headed in often contradictory directions."

—Robert Ellwood, emeritus professor of religion, University of Southern California

A MERICAN RELIGION flourishes in a consumer culture, and presents us with a bewildering array of choices as we navigate the shopping mall of faith. The authors identify dozens of trends that will shape American religion in the next century and bring together the latest research and intimate portraits of Americans describing their beliefs, their religious heritage, and their spiritual search. With warmth and style the authors document how consumerism shapes religious practice—from conservative evangelical worship to the most esoteric New Age workshop.

Shopping for Faith is more than a book, it is an open line. Its companion CD-ROM enables readers to monitor religious trends via the Internet. Containing the book's entire text, fully searchable and keyword hotlinked, the *Shopping for Faith* CD-ROM connects readers from key terms in the book to resources on the World Wide Web. These web resources—links to related sites and current news stories—are researched and maintained by TheLinkLibrary.com. This innovative feature is sure to keep you apprised of the latest offerings in America's spiritual supermarket well into this new century.

RICHARD CIMINO is editor and publisher of the much-quoted newsletter, *Religion Watch* (http://www.religionwatch.com), which researches trends in contemporary religion. He has worked extensively as a researcher and freelance writer for various publications, including *Christian Century* and *Religion News Service*. He is the author of *Against the Stream: The Adoption of Christian Faiths by Young Adults.*

DON LATTIN is the award-winning religion writer for the San Francisco *Chronicle*. Over the past twenty years he has interviewed thousands of Americans about their religious heritage and spiritual search. He was a fellow at the Program in Religious Studies for Journalists at the University of North Carolina at Chapel Hill and has also taught religion reporting at the Graduate School of Journalism at the University of California at Berkeley. *(Price subject to change)*

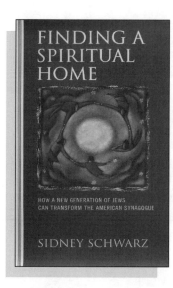

Finding a Spiritual Home

How a New Generation of Jews Can Transform the American Synagogue

Sidney Schwarz

$24.00 Hardcover
ISBN 0-7879-5174-9

"An extraordinary book. A clarion call for spiritual leadership in a post-ethnic age."

—RABBI LAWRENCE A. HOFFMAN, Hebrew Union College, New York; co-founder, Synagogue 2000: Institute for the Synagogue of the Twenty-First Century

"With stories both of individuals and synagogues, Sidney Schwarz shows that old religious structures can indeed become alive with new spiritual meaning, sensitive to generational change. His is an encouraging, beautifully written account of congregations in positive transition—at once inspiring and instructive."

—WADE CLARK ROOF, J.F. Rowny professor of religion and society, University of California at Santa Barbara; author of *A Generation of Seekers: The Spiritual Journeys of the Baby Boom Generation* and *Spiritual Marketplace*

L IKE COUNTLESS others of their generation, many post-war American Jews have abandoned the religion of their birth to search for a spiritual home in other traditions. Some find their way back to the faith of their heritage, but why do so many find that the synagogue has not met their needs?

In this illuminating look at Judaism's future, Rabbi Sidney Schwarz offers a penetrating analysis of the American Jewish community, challenging American synagogues to respond to a generation of seekers and satisfy the spiritual hunger of the "new American Jew." This groundbreaking book not only reveals the possibilities of this new, vital spiritual culture, but also offers strategies for transforming any congregation into a place that the Jews of today can truly call home.

An added bonus in the book is a discussion guide for book clubs and study groups.

SIDNEY SCHWARZ is the founder and president of The Washington Institute for Jewish Leadership and Values, an educational foundation dedicated to renewal of American Jewish life through Judaic study, social justice, and civic activism. He is the founding rabbi of Adat Shalom Reconstructionist Congregation in Bethesda, MD and the author of two books and numerous articles on contemporary Jewish life.

(Price subject to change)

Virtual Faith

The Irreverent Spiritual Quest of Generation X

Tom Beaudoin
Foreword by Harvey Cox

$23.95 Hardcover
ISBN 0-7879-3882-3

$16.00 Paperback
ISBN 0-7879-5527-2

"Reveals the deep and pervasive search for meaning that haunts Generation X. This book is must reading for anyone who would understand the spirituality of young people at the turn of a new millennium."

—ROBERT A. LUDWIG, author of *Reconstructing Catholicism for a New Generation*

IN *Virtual Faith*, Tom Beaudoin explores fashion, music videos, and cyberspace concluding that his generation has fashioned a theology radically different from, but no less potent or valid than, that of their elders. Beaudoin's investigation of popular culture uncovers four themes that underpin his generation's theology. First, all institutions are suspect—especially organized religion. Second, personal experience is everything, and every form of intense personal experience is potentially spiritual. Third, suffering is also spiritual. Finally, this generation sees ambiguity as a central element of faith.

This book opens a long overdue conversation about where and how we find meaning, and how we all can encourage each other in this central human searching. Parents and religious leaders of all religious persuasions will gain an understanding of GenX theology in its own terms. And GenXers themselves will find an invitation to a more conscious examination of their own relationship to religion and spiritual experience—and a challenge to take the next step.

TOM BEAUDOIN earned his Master of Theological Studies from Harvard University School of Divinity in 1996 and his Ph.D. in Religion and Education at Boston College.

(Price subject to change)

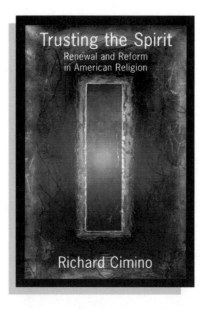

Trusting the Spirit

Renewal and Reform in American Religion

Richard Cimino

$21.95 Hardcover
ISBN: 0787951609

"Richard Cimino's well-researched case studies add immensely to our awareness of the substantial and increasing vigor of American religion. His book comes as another compelling rebuke to those still clinging to the passé claim that religion is declining and must soon die."

—RODNEY STARK, professor of sociology and comparative religion, University of Washington

Trusting the Spirit is an in-depth look at a range of current reform and renewal movements in traditional denominations that reveals what is—and is not—working to revitalize the institutions and spiritual lives of American Christians and Jews. As mainstream denominations struggle to retain members and also remain vibrant communities of faith, renewal and reform have emerged as important topics. *Trusting the Spirit* examines the main components of the renewal and reform process, describes their dynamics, and reveals how effective these organizations and movements have been within their traditions.

Going beyond description of these new organizations, Richard Cimino's journalistic approach takes readers inside each group to analyze their effectiveness in achieving their goals of spiritual and institutional change. Using interviews, observation, case studies, and analysis, Cimino shows how all the components of renewal and reform—the organization, the larger denomination, the congregation, and the individual members—interact at both local and national levels.

RICHARD CIMINO is editor and publisher of the much-quoted newsletter, *Religion Watch* (http://www.religionwatch.com), which researches trends in contemporary religion. He has worked extensively as a researcher and freelance writer for various publications, including *Christian Century* and Religion News Service. He is the author of *Against the Stream: The Adoption of Christian Faiths by Young Adults,* and co-author with Don Lattin of the groundbreaking *Shopping for Faith: American Religion in the New Millennium.*   *(Price subject to change)*